"James Emery White has done a masterful job of explaining discipleship for new and seasoned believers alike. Often the great books on discipleship are deep but inaccessible. Others are easy to read but lack depth. Jim takes a wealth of knowledge and insight on the essentials of Christian discipleship and makes them wonderfully easy to understand but deep enough to authentically help you."

Carey Nieuwhof, leadership author, podcaster, and founding pastor of Connexus Church in Barrie, Ontario

"Living a life with Christ is not a onetime commitment. White reminds us it is a lifetime of intentional choices and disciplined practices that help us in our desire to be followers of Jesus."

Suzanne Stabile, author of *The Path between Us*, coauthor of *The Road Back to You*, and host of *The Enneagram Journey* podcast

"I have long loved the writings of James Emery White for his unique insights into the Christian faith and his knack for unraveling complex issues. Now he offers us an updated, refreshing guide for following Jesus in a confusing and sometimes hostile world. *After "I Believe"* is a practical resource for spiritual growth. Compellingly straightforward, this book will help you align yourself to biblical truth to effect real life-change. Jim's chapter on prayer alone makes this book worth buying. If you want to inject your Christian life with a good dose of adventure and wonder, then you'll want to read this book."

Skip Heitzig, pastor of Calvary Church in Albuquerque, New Mexico, and author of *The Bible from 30,000 Feet*

"In *After 'I Believe*,' Ja⎯⎯⎯⎯⎯⎯⎯⎯⎯⎯⎯ rilliant understanding of profoi⎯⎯⎯⎯⎯⎯⎯⎯⎯⎯⎯ ove and lead people toward a li⎯⎯⎯⎯⎯⎯⎯⎯⎯⎯⎯ It lights the way for anyone seel⎯⎯⎯⎯⎯⎯⎯⎯⎯⎯⎯ g life to the fullest as God intended."

Santiago "Jimmy" Mellado, president and CEO of Compassion International

AFTER "I BELIEVE"

AFTER
"I BELIEVE"

EVERYDAY PRACTICES
FOR A VIBRANT FAITH

JAMES EMERY WHITE

BakerBooks
a division of Baker Publishing Group
Grand Rapids, Michigan

© 2021 by James Emery White

Published by Baker Books
a division of Baker Publishing Group
PO Box 6287, Grand Rapids, MI 49516-6287
www.bakerbooks.com

Printed in the United States of America

Library of Congress Cataloging-in-Publication Data
Names: White, James Emery, 1961– author.
Title: After "I believe" : everyday practices for a vibrant faith / James Emery White.
Description: Grand Rapids, Michigan : Baker Books, a division of Baker Publishing Group, 2021.
Identifiers: LCCN 2020023163 | ISBN 9780801094606 (paperback)
Subjects: LCSH: Christian life. | Spiritual formation.
Classification: LCC BV4501.3 .W465 2021 | DDC 248.4—dc23
LC record available at https://lccn.loc.gov/2020023163

ISBN 978-1-5409-0143-9 (casebound)

21   22   23   24   25   26   27   7   6   5   4   3   2   1

CONTENTS

ACKNOWLEDGMENTS

I wish to thank the Baker team for their support of this project, our eighth together, and specifically Bob Hosack, who agreed to swapping out our original idea for another very late in the game.

Alli Main continues to serve my life and maintain my deepest gratitude for co-laboring on all of my writing. Whether through research or editing, feedback or ideas, constructive criticism or encouragement, she is nothing less than a godsend—which means a special thanks to her husband, Keith, as well.

And as always, my wife, Susan, continues to make every page possible in countless ways. Going on forty years of marriage at the time of this writing, my debt to her knows no bounds.

INTRODUCTION

Are you tired? Worn out? Burned out on religion? Come to me. Get away with me and you'll recover your life. I'll show you how to take a real rest. Walk with me and work with me—watch how I do it. Learn the unforced rhythms of grace. I won't lay anything heavy or ill-fitting on you. Keep company with me and you'll learn to live freely and lightly.—Jesus, Matthew 11:28–30

When I was twenty years old, I had several close friends who knew I was very, very far from God, but they cared about me. I remember how one night when we were together, one of them told me the story of their faith journey to Christ. It came out very naturally in the course of our conversation together. It was interesting, parts of it were convicting, and (admittedly) parts were uncomfortable at times. What was clear was that I wasn't ready. They would invite me to church or to a campus Christian ministry they were a part of, and I would always say no.

I had been raised by a PhD father and a schoolteacher mother. Reading and books, intellectual conversations and debate had been the wallpaper of my life. In our family, Christianity as a belief system was embraced, though we were largely unchurched throughout my childhood. I would have told you I was a Christian because of what I believed, but I wasn't one based on how I behaved. The divide between knowing and doing, believing and behaving—the idea of Savior and the reality of Lord—was stark. There were moments this was revealed to me in very pointed ways. For example, one late night in college, after more than my fair share of beer or whiskey or whatever my choice had been for that night, I got into a debate with someone who was a Mormon. I've always been disciplined about research and study, and I loved to debate people. We were talking, and I was slicing and dicing through the historicity and theology of his religion. He remained silent until I was done with my tirade and then had just one question for me in response: "How can you say anything to me about what's right or wrong with how you live?"

He was right. It stung, but not enough.

Then I went through a summer that was . . . awful. The details aren't important, but I hit rock bottom in all kinds of ways. For the first time in my life, I was open to God, open to spiritual things—just open to change. I didn't like where my life was heading. At the start of the new school year, friends again invited me to go to a campus Christian ministry meeting with them. You could have knocked them over with a feather when I said okay.

It was a disarming experience. There were two hundred or more students there, and students I recognized. Athletes, people from student government, people I knew from class. Normal people. People I knew and liked and respected. The music was not like anything I had ever heard in church the few times I went as a kid. It was led by students playing guitars and came dangerously close to actually having a beat.

Then came the talk.

A twenty-something leader served up Jesus and the Christian faith raw and unfiltered. It was direct, challenging, and clear. I was talked to and with—not at. And it was on what I needed more than anything—someone confronting me directly about where I stood with God in terms of both head and heart. At the end, there was a challenge to accept that for my life—for Christ to be my Leader and Forgiver.

I did. I went home on cloud nine. I had truly crossed the line of faith. There was actually a lot I didn't know. I knew a fair amount about Christ, a disproportionate amount for a new Christian, but virtually nothing about the Christ *life*.

This is a book for those who have crossed the line of faith and become a Christian on how to become Christlike. To truly engage the Christ *life*. To *grow* in that faith. It is a companion to *Christianity for People Who Aren't Christians*, a book designed to help those exploring the Christian faith for their life. This book is designed to help those who have chosen Christianity as their faith to develop themselves spiritually in light of that choice. This is not unlike developing yourself physically. If you want to develop your physical life, you invest in exercises, activities, and pursuits that will develop your body. Developing a spiritual life also involves certain exercises. You will find these exercises, along with other activities and relationships, experiences and investments, in each chapter.

There is an important distinction, though, between spiritual development and other areas of self-improvement. If I work out to improve my physical life, I am *being* physical. If I engage in a book discussion group to develop myself intellectually, I am *being* intellectual. Not so with our spiritual life: Spiritual exercises are *not* the same as *being* spiritual. By themselves, spiritual activities lead to nothing but lifeless religion. The heart of authentic Christian spirituality is relational, not institutional, nor—a surprise to many—simply experiential. True Christian spirituality is intimacy with God and an ongoing transformation into the likeness of Christ. In other words, much of what we will explore together are the means to an end—a deeper, more intimate relationship with God through Jesus.

I had many people invest in my own journey of spiritual growth and life as a follower of Christ. It is my hope and prayer that this book, in some small way, pays their investment forward.

CHAPTER ONE

IDENTITIES, DECEPTIONS, AND MYTHS

The words "You are my Beloved" reveal the most intimate truth about all human beings. —Henri J. M. Nouwen[1]

New.

It's an amazing word, and there's rarely a time we don't like it. A new car, a new year, a new baby, a new . . . you. That's the promise of the Christian life. A new *you.* The way Paul describes this in his letter to the Corinthian church in the New Testament almost bristles with excitement: "Anyone who belongs to Christ has become a new person. The old life is gone; a new life has begun! And all of this is a gift from God, who brought us back to himself through Christ" (2 Cor. 5:17–18 NLT).

Your Identities in Christ

Understanding this newness is at the heart of developing your life in Christ. If you do not understand your new identity and new position, you will never be able to grow into who you have been called to be. Your new life in Christ *is* this new identity. And it begins with your new identity as a child of God.

You Are Adopted

When you became a Christian, you entered into that relationship with God through adoption. You became a son or daughter. That is who you are in Christ. In the book of John, the Bible says, "Yet to all who did receive him [Christ], to those who believed in his name, he gave the right to become children of God" (1:12). In Galatians, we read, "For you are all children of God through faith in Christ Jesus" (3:26 NLT). This is important. When we come to God, we aren't just saved from some kind of punishment, given a set of creeds and doctrines, or given our marching orders and told to fall into line. We are adopted into his family as children!

Now, in one sense, Christian or not, we are all God's children. He created all of us and he loves all of us. But when we live apart from him, we break off that relationship and, as a result, separate ourselves from God. It's as if we abandon the family and legally change our last name. But as Christians, we have received forgiveness for anything we have ever done that is wrong or hurtful in God's eyes and have come home and entered into the intimacy of God's love for us as Father to child. We then continually drink from that forgiveness and acceptance and grace. We have become adopted, welcomed back, into his family. We have come home and become who we were meant to be—prized sons and precious daughters in an intimate relationship with our Father God.

When we come to God as Father through Jesus, we hear from God the same thing Jesus heard as his Son. Did you know that? When you emerge from the waters of baptism, the Father says the same thing to you he said to his Son, Jesus, at his baptism: "And a voice from heaven said, 'You are my dearly loved Son, and you bring me great joy'" (Luke 3:22 NLT). David Taylor writes that this is our baptism name. We are named "The loved one—Beloved." Of all the things God could have said about the Son, he said, "You are the beloved." And when we are baptized in Jesus's name, we hear the same whisper from the Father, calling us our truest name: the loved one.[2]

Being a son or a daughter isn't just a title—it becomes the very beating of God's heart toward us. Or as the apostle John wrote, "Consider the incredible love that the Father has shown us in allowing us to be called 'children of God'—and that is not just what we are called, but what we *are*" (1 John 3:1 Phillips, emphasis mine). There's nothing you can ever do to make him love you more, and there's nothing you can ever do to make him love you less. As the apostle Paul taught, "May you be able to feel and understand, as all God's children should, how long, how wide, how deep, and how high his love really is; and to experience this love for yourselves, though it is so great that you will never see the end of it or fully know or understand it" (Eph. 3:18–19 TLB).

> *"Consider the incredible love that the Father has shown us in allowing us to be called 'children of God'—and that is not just what we are called, but what we are"* (1 John 3:1 Phillips).

But that's not all. Not only does God offer us that identity, he wants us to live in light of it. This is key, because a change in identity doesn't mean anything if it isn't allowed to speak to how you actually live. God wants us to *live* as sons and daughters, and to let that new identity form the deepest understanding of who we are and how we relate to him! Again, being a son or a daughter isn't just a title—it's a new status. It's how you can now *relate* to God—how you are *supposed* to relate to God.

Jesus went out of his way to teach this, to show that this is how relating to God was meant to be. We see an example of this in how he taught his followers to pray. Back in Jesus's day, many of the varying religious sects and groups were *known* by how they prayed. That is how they were marked. So it was very natural for the followers of Jesus to say, "So what kind of pray-ers are we?

What will mark us when we pray? What defines our movement? Teach us." Jesus agreed and said, "This is how you should talk to God the Father." Then he gave them the suggested outline. It was not a verbatim set of words to parrot back. It was similar to "Pray like this . . . pray along these lines." It was more the *way* to talk to God, the things you should talk to God about. And it began in a most startling way: "Our Father in heaven." When Jesus began with that, the mouths of the people listening dropped open. If they were standing they surely sat down. It may have been the most startling thing they had heard from him to that point.

Why? Because he used the Aramaic word *Abba* for "Father." No one had ever used that word for God before, much less as a way of addressing him. This was spiritual history being made. *Abba* was the most intimate family term there was, used between a very small child and their parent.[3] In contemporary English, it has often been suggested that the best translation would be "Daddy." Some linguists even go so far as to say it should be translated "DaDa," like the very first words that a baby might say while being held in the arms of their father.

His point? We should live and talk and interact and grow in our relationship with God in just this way. As the apostle Paul wrote, "For all who are led by the Spirit of God are children of God. So you have not received a spirit that makes you fearful slaves. Instead, you received God's Spirit when he adopted you as his own children. Now we call him, 'Abba, Father'" (Rom. 8:14–15 NLT).

You Are a Saint

But you are more than a son or a daughter. As his child, God has also declared you to be a saint. If you are in a relationship with Christ as your Forgiver and Leader, you have been declared, positionally, by God, to be a saint. He now wants you to become what you have been named.

This idea of sainthood was so clear to the early church that it was one of the most common ways for them to refer to each other. They would call each other saints. Notice how the apostle Paul opened his letter to the church at Ephesus: "From Paul, an apostle of Christ Jesus by the will of God, to the *saints* [in Ephesus]" (Eph. 1:1 NET, emphasis mine). He didn't say to the "people" in Ephesus or the "church" in Ephesus, but the *saints* in Ephesus.

I know, you don't feel much like a saint. Neither do I. Saints are supposed to be these holy, almost-perfect people who have committed their entire life to doing the work of God in a spirit of humility under great persecution. Not many of us fit that bill. You may have even come from a background where saints were figures from history that the church recognized as people to be venerated, even prayed to. So what does it mean that those of us who are Christ followers are called saints? And not just some of us, but all of us?

The word *saint* means "those who are set apart," meaning someone who has been freed from the chains of sin, not to mention the consequences of sin. Biblically, a saint is someone who has been made holy. The moment you trust Christ, coming to him for forgiveness and leadership, the very nature of your spiritual state is radically altered. God's forgiveness moves you from a state where you are under the full weight and penalty of your sin, to a state where that weight and penalty has been removed. This is what becoming a Christ follower—becoming a Christian—is all about. It's not about getting your act together. It's not about following a bunch of dos and don'ts. It's about accepting this radical gift of forgiveness that you could never earn and never deserve. It's letting what Jesus did on the cross begin the transforming work in you—letting his death take the place of your death, his sinlessness cover your sinfulness.

When you become a Christian, God has a very clear agenda for your life: it's to make you like Jesus.

God doesn't just declare us saints positionally; he also wants to develop us into saints *functionally*. When you become a Christian, God has a very clear agenda for your life: it's to make you like Jesus. It's to take your life and have you become the person he has declared you to be. It's as if God says, "You're a saint—now live like one! Let's start the process and go to work." But that's not all. He also says, "And I'll show you the way."

Imagine if Michael Jordan, the greatest player in NBA history and now owner of the Charlotte Hornets, came to you and said, "You're on my team. You are now officially a member of the Charlotte Hornets basketball team. Here's your uniform and your locker. It's official. You are now a Hornet."

Jordan then goes on to say, "And don't worry—your status as a member of the team has nothing to do with your basketball ability. I am just choosing to accept you, to bestow this identity upon you. You are a Hornet. But here's what I want to do: now that you are on an NBA team, I want you to let me develop you into a professional-level player. I want you to become who I have declared you to be."

So let's explore how to become the saint God has declared you to be as his child. But first, we have to name some deadly deceptions and do away with some spiritual myths.

Deadly Deceptions

If you are going to understand the nature of almost all deceptions related to spiritual growth and development, you will need to understand that, in truth, there's no such thing as a spiritual life. There's just life, and it's meant to be lived spiritually. That's not particularly original with me. It's been the headline for what the Christ life is all about for more than two thousand years. The very word *Christian* means "little Christ," meaning someone who is living like Jesus lived. So your spiritual life is not a compartment or area of your existence. It's meant to permeate every fiber of your being.

The great spiritual deception is thinking that the *appearance* of spirituality is spirituality itself. I once heard of an eastern holy man who covered himself with ashes as a sign of humility and regularly sat on a prominent street corner in his city. When tourists asked permission to take his picture, he would rearrange the ashes to create the best image of destitution and humility. Was that true humility? Was that true spirituality? Of course not. But you'd be surprised how many people fall into this trap—not in crass, hypocritical ways like rearranging their ashes to look like they're closer to God, but in well-intentioned ways, confusing appearance with reality.

Two substitutes for authentic spirituality are the deadliest.

The Deception of Religion

The first of these deadly deceptions is religious activity, or just religion itself. The deception of religion is thinking that when we go through certain religious rites, rituals, or membership processes, or when we attend certain services or ceremonies, we are being spiritual. The more revealing name for this is *legalism*.

As I have written before, legalism is putting a bunch of dos and don'ts on people to follow, in the name of God, that God did not say they needed to follow.[4] It's a religion of added rules and regulations, standards and stipulations, codes and conduct, contrived by someone to determine who is, or who is not, spiritual. It's being asked—if not forced—to measure up in a way that can be binding and brutal, discouraging and defeating. It rightly feels about a million miles away from anything authentic, anything life-changing, anything . . . freeing.

Legalism is actually what set up the tension between Jesus and the religious leaders of his day—the "teachers of the law" and the group known as the Pharisees. They were very religious and considered to be the holiest people of the day. They took the Old Testament and calculated that it contained 248 commandments and 365 prohibitions, and they lifted those out and vowed to obey every single one. To make sure that they didn't break one of those rules, they made rules about the rules they made and laws about the laws! In fact, they came up with more than 1,500 additions.

Christianity is not about religion, it's about a relationship.

So how do rules about rules about rules play out? To avoid taking the Lord's name in vain, they refused to ever say God's name, even in honor and respect, worship and prayer. To avoid committing adultery, they would lower their heads whenever they passed a woman so that they wouldn't even look at her, because if they looked they might lust. This is why the most holy of all were known as "bleeding Pharisees" because they were lowering their heads so much they were always running into walls.[5] To properly follow the command to rest on the Sabbath and not work, they decided they needed to figure out how many steps you could take on those days without it becoming labor. For whatever reason, they calculated that to travel beyond about a half mile on the Sabbath was work and, therefore, violated the law. They also decided that on holy days, a person could eat but not cook, could bandage a wounded person but not apply medicine. And if you were a woman, you couldn't look in the mirror because you might see a gray hair, and if you saw a gray hair you might be tempted to pluck it out, and plucking out a gray hair was considered work, and you couldn't work on the Sabbath.[6]

But Christianity is not about religion, much less its accompanying seduction into legalism; it's about a relationship.

The Deception of Knowledge

A second deception related to spiritual growth and development is the deceit of knowledge. This is the idea that all you need is to know and believe the right things: intellectual assent—embracing Christianity on a philosophical level. But knowledge alone is meaningless. I can believe in a lot of things, but that doesn't mean those beliefs impact my life, much less reflect my life. As Thomas Kelly once observed, the heart of spirituality has less to do with "knowledge about" than it does "acquaintance with."[7]

I spent about three weeks in Moscow in the spring of 1994 at the Moscow Theological Institute as part of a teaching team that went to work with Russian pastors who had never received any theological, biblical, or pastoral training. It was an interesting time to go to Russia. It had been only a few years since the fall of Communism, under which Christianity had been outlawed and Christians had been routinely persecuted and imprisoned. Freedom was something new and something not wholly trusted to last. Many of my students still bore the scars and serial-number tattoos from the gulags and prisons where they were imprisoned for their faith. One of the churches I spoke at was a former underground house church that had met and worshiped together secretly for years under Communist rule. Their faith was deep, infectious, and authentic.

I once read of a similar house church that met in small groups at night throughout the week in order to avoid arousing the suspicion of the KGB informers. One of the underground small groups began to softly sing a hymn together, when suddenly two soldiers walked in, pointed their guns at the group, and announced, "If you wish to renounce your commitment to Jesus Christ, leave now!" Two or three of the members of the group quickly left and, after a few more seconds, two more.

Then one of the soldiers looked at the remaining group, pointed his rifle, and said, "This is your last chance. Either turn against your faith in Christ or stay and suffer the consequences." And when he said that, he pulled the bolt back on his gun to make it ready for fire. Two more people slipped out into the night. No one else moved, including parents with small children trembling by their side, each one expecting to be gunned down or imprisoned. Then one of the soldiers shut the door, looked back at those who stood against the wall, and said, "Keep your hands up—but this time in praise to God. We too are Christians. But we have learned that unless people are willing to die for their faith, they cannot be fully trusted."[8]

Whenever I think of that story, I am reminded that many people claim to believe in Jesus, but true belief is more than just saying that you accept the facts. Believing is giving your life over to what you say you believe. Believing is commitment. In very direct terms, James, the half brother of Jesus, wrote, "Does merely talking about faith indicate that a person really has it? . . . Do I hear you professing to believe in the one and only God, but then observe you complacently sitting back as if you had done something wonderful? That's just great. Demons do that, but what good does it do them? Use your heads!" (James 2:14, 19 MSG).

So how do you experience an authentically spiritual life, one that results in real life change that reflects the Jesus you follow? Now that we've addressed the deceptions, let's clear away the myths.

The Myths of Spiritual Growth

Comedian Yakov Smirnoff immigrated to the United States in 1977 not knowing any English. He joked that when he first came to the United States from Russia, he wasn't prepared for the incredible variety of instant products available in American grocery stores. "I'll never forget walking down one of the aisles (of the grocery store) and seeing powdered milk; just add water and you get milk. Right next to it was powdered orange juice; just add water and you get orange juice. Then I saw baby powder, and I thought to myself, *What a country!*"[9]

The Instantaneous Myth

The first misunderstanding about the nature of the spiritual life is that spirituality happens—instantly—at the moment you enter into a relationship with God. This false belief is that when you give your life to Christ, you experience an immediate, substantive, in-depth miraculous change in habits, attitudes, and character. Just add God, and you get a spiritual life. The truth is that entering into a relationship with God does nothing more than begin the ongoing development of that relationship.

C. S. Lewis explored the intricacies of spiritual growth in his masterful work *The Screwtape Letters* under the guise of correspondence between two demons over their "patient" on earth. Early on in the book, the human who had been the demons' subject of temptation becomes a Christian. The elder demon, named Screwtape, counsels his young nephew, Wormwood, not to despair, saying, "All the habits of the patient, both mental and bodily, are still in our favour."[10] The insight of Lewis's Screwtape is profound. Deep, lasting life change does not often happen at the moment your relationship with God begins. The Holy Spirit can do whatever he wishes, but even the most casual of observers would quickly note that he hasn't often desired to work instantaneous, miraculous life change in a new believer's life.

When you begin your relationship with God, your eternal destiny is altered and you experience a radical reorientation of priorities, a new life purpose, and the power of God in your life. But rather than instant communion with God at the deepest of levels,

Rather than the immediate liberation from every bad habit or character flaw you've ever possessed, the experience is more like an army that lands on a beachhead and then begins routing out the enemy as it moves inland.

you experience the beginning of a new relationship that develops in intimacy and depth over time. And rather than the immediate liberation from every bad habit or character flaw you've ever possessed, the experience is more like an army that lands on a beachhead and then begins routing out the enemy as it moves inland. This is why the Bible instructs Christians to "let your roots grow down into him and draw up nourishment from him. See that you go on growing in the Lord, and become strong and vigorous in the truth you were taught" (Col. 2:7 TLB). The language is important. You have to *let* your roots grow; you have to *draw up* nourishment; you have to *keep on* growing; you have to *become* strong and vigorous. Spirituality isn't something that just happens; it's something to be nurtured, and you have to be intentional about that nurturing. Becoming a Christian is just the beginning of the journey; it's the start of a life that follows Christ. That life is meant to deepen and grow. As Richard Foster has written, "Superficiality is the curse of our age. . . . The desperate need today is not for a greater number of intelligent people, or gifted people, but for deep people."[11]

The Time Myth

Yet while Christianity is a journey, it is not *merely* a journey. Another myth is that true spirituality is simply a by-product of time. Being a Christian does not automatically translate into becoming Christlike. This is why a five-year-old Christian will not necessarily have five years' worth of spiritual maturity. This is a very important dynamic to understand, so let's come at it in a different way to drive it home.

I first picked up the game of golf when I was in graduate school. I took two lessons from a course pro, bought a set of the cheapest clubs I could find (I did mention I was in graduate school), and began to play. Initially, I made quick progress. But then I began to play with less and less frequency. Soon, I only played at the annual Christmas gathering with my wife's family. As you might expect, I played about the same each year—translation, it was rough (and in the rough)—because I hadn't played since the previous year. I have since started to play with more regularity, and my game has improved. But if someone were to ask me how long I've played, the answer would be deceiving. I could tell them I've played for more than three decades, but that doesn't mean anything because I haven't been intentional about my game during that time. People who have been playing only a year but have developed their game through lessons and practice could easily outplay me.

This is a crucial understanding. I can subscribe to golf magazines, purchase golf equipment, live by a golf course, wear golf clothing, watch golf on TV, and hang out at the golf clubhouse and never improve my game! Simply being exposed to something has little bearing on whether we become proficient at it. Again, while your spirituality takes time, it is not simply a by-product of time.

The writer of the book of Hebrews told a group of Christians that "though by this time you ought to be teachers, you need someone to teach you the elementary truths of God's word all over again" (5:12). That stings, but it's true. I can be exposed to any number of Christians and dynamics of Christian culture but not be affected by them. Yet I can be deceived into thinking I have been.

The Effort Myth

Another myth is that spiritual growth is attained through effort. The idea is that people must simply decide to be spiritual, as though spiritual living is essentially an act of the will. Love, joy, peace, patience, kindness, goodness, faithfulness, gentleness, and self-control are believed to be matters of *effort*. While spiritual development demands intentionality, merely trying to experience life change can never bring about life change. Again, let's come at it from a different angle to ensure we don't miss the nature of this myth.

I mentioned Michael Jordan earlier. A whole generation of basketball players grew up wanting to "be like Mike." While names like LeBron, Kobe, Steph, and Zion have since emerged, few deny that Michael was arguably the greatest of all time. People still want to shoot like he did, jump like he did, jam like he did and, most importantly, have their tongue hang out like he did. And they try!

Hard! But few come even close to mirroring Jordan's level of play. Why? Because you don't play like Jordan by trying; you play to his level by *training*. And not just any training, but the training regimen he followed to play the way he played.[12]

The heart of Christian spirituality is to be like Jesus. To be like Jesus you don't merely try either—you train. You do the things Jesus did in order to live like Jesus lived. That's why Jesus once said that "everyone who is fully trained will be like their teacher" (Luke 6:40). Or as the apostle Paul wrote, "Train yourself to be godly" (1 Tim. 4:7). "Anyone who is not a continual student of Jesus, and who nevertheless reads the great promises of the Bible as if they were for him or her," writes Dallas Willard, "is like someone trying to cash a check on another person's account."[13] The key to a spiritual life is to order your life around those activities, disciplines, and practices that were modeled by Christ in order to accomplish through training what you cannot do by trying.[14]

The Solo Myth

A fourth myth is that a *personal* relationship with God through Christ is synonymous with a *private* relationship with God through Christ. Think about the following phrases:

"It's not what you know, but who you know."

"It pays to be well-connected."

"It takes having friends in high places."

"She has a great support network."

"He's got a good supporting cast."

"They were well coached."

Then there's the opposite:

"I don't think he had anyone helping him."

"Nobody had his back."

"She didn't know the right people."

"He tried to do it by himself."

What do all of these sayings point to? One thing: the power of people in our life. Sadly, a recent LifeWay study found that less than half of all Christians active in church spend time with other believers to help them grow in their faith.[15] The younger the age, the more individualistic they are. Two-thirds say they don't need anyone in their life to help them walk with God. The truth, however, is that becoming a truly spiritual person is a team sport.

This insight is taught throughout the Bible. In Proverbs, we read that "as iron sharpens iron, so one man sharpens another" (27:17). The writer of Hebrews said, "Let us consider how we may spur one another on toward love and good deeds, not giving up meeting together, as some are in the habit of doing, but encouraging one another" (10:24–25). Throughout the Bible, in the lives of those who developed their faith in God, you see strategic relationships. Jethro mentored his son-in-law, Moses. Moses then turned around and made a relational contribution to the life of his successor, Joshua. The prophet Elijah poured his life into Elisha. Mary, the mother of Jesus, turned to her older cousin, Elizabeth. And Jesus set apart twelve men in order to invest his life into theirs. His disciples followed suit, with Paul taking Timothy under his wing, and Barnabas and Peter doing the same for Mark. Investing through relationship was the anvil on which spiritual growth was forged.

> "As iron sharpens iron, so one man sharpens another" (Prov. 27:17).

The Transformation Myth

The final myth is one you will want to continually remind yourself of throughout the course of your life. Let's call it the transformation myth. This is the idea that transformation is an achievement, or something you attain. Like a light switch, once you turn it on, it's on. The truth is that your spiritual growth will often be a process of three steps forward, two steps back. This has been called the "law of undulation." To *undulate* means to move in waves, to go up and down in terms of your progress. This is simply the normal process when it comes to the flow of our spiritual lives. It is the nearest thing we humans have to normalcy.[16]

Not only is this true in terms of actual spiritual growth, but also in terms of how you actually *feel*. Many people believe that true spirituality is gauged by feeling. Do I *feel* close to God? Do I *feel* spiritual? The reality is that authentic spirituality, while a dynamic enterprise that involves your entire being, has more to do with how you respond to your emotions than it does with your current emotional state. There will be times you feel up or down, high or low but, in truth, your feelings may have very little to do with the actual state of where you are with God. The state of your spirituality does not rest on how you feel, but on who you are—and who you are becoming.

The state of your spirituality does not rest on how you feel, but on who you are—and who you are becoming.

All to say, God is in the soul-making business, and he does promise to transform you! You don't have to transform yourself or generate feelings of transformation. As God said through the prophet Ezekiel, "I will give you a new heart and put a new spirit in you; I will remove from you your heart of stone and give you a heart of flesh" (Ezek. 36:26).

Becoming a Disciple

The key idea is becoming a disciple. In Christian circles, we often talk of "discipling" someone, "being" discipled, or going to a church where there is a strong emphasis on discipleship. The problem is that most of the time, that means going where you will be spoon-fed or bottle-fed. Where someone is actively teaching while you are passively taking notes. Someone is discipling you, which means how it affects you is based on whether they are a good discipler, or whether the church is effective in terms of discipleship. In other words, discipleship is something you receive.

This is why people talk about being fed or complain that they aren't being fed. Discipleship isn't really about them, it's about something that happens *to* them. There is an active discipleship force and they are the passive recipients. But if that's the way it works, why aren't more people like the disciples we read about in the Bible, particularly when, in truth, there is greater access to gifted teachers (online) than ever before?

Our confusion stems from the fact that this is not what discipleship is about. The word *disciple* is from the Greek word *mathetes* and literally means "learner." You can only be a learner if you are the one doing the learning. The point is that you, as a disciple—as a learner—are to be actively engaged in learning. It is *your* responsibility to take up the mantle of self-development.

Think about how this worked with Jesus. He invited a very select group of men and women to do life with him for approximately thirty-six months. Formally, there were the twelve disciples, but there were also women such as Mary, Martha, and Mary Magdalene whom he invested in as well. Theirs was an invitation to learn—not to enter into a passive process of being fed. We certainly know that not all of the twelve took this invitation to heart; one in particular didn't seem to learn much of anything. If discipleship was simply something "done" to you or for you, Jesus failed epically as a discipler with Judas. Anyone want to say that Jesus was not a good discipler? Then get that understanding of discipleship out of your head.

Here's the truth about being a learner: growing spiritually is something that can be served by other people but ultimately must be owned personally by you. Too many followers of Christ view discipleship as something that is done to them and for them, almost like a personal enrichment program or getting a life coach. No. That's why in the New Testament book of Hebrews we're told that people who keep looking to get "fed" are in a state of arrested development. They're like babies who never grow up, always wanting their bottle. If you think I'm being sarcastic in how I paraphrase it, read it yourself:

> We have much to say about this, but it is hard to make it clear to you because you no longer try to understand. In fact, though by this time you ought to be teachers, you need someone to teach you the elementary truths of God's word all over again. You need milk, not solid food! Anyone who lives on milk, being still an infant, is not acquainted with the teaching about righteousness. But solid food is for the mature, who by constant use have *trained themselves* to distinguish good from evil. (Heb. 5:11–14, emphasis mine)

Growing in your faith is not about finding the best teaching, making sure you land in the best small group, and taking the best classes or seminars you can. Those are all fine add-ons, but the heart of the challenge is for you to become an active, self-motivated, self-feeding learner.

First Steps

So how do you begin to change? If transformation is not instantaneous nor merely a product of time, how do you enter into training? Two ways will provide the backdrop for the rest of this book: cooperation and investment. Let's begin with cooperation.

Cooperation

One of the ways I worked my way through graduate school was by coaching basketball. Some of the kids on my team had incredible talent and seemingly unlimited potential. I knew that if they would follow what I said, and follow much better coaches than me in the years to come, they could channel that skill and talent into a team effort on the court, and begin a path that could take them all the way to college competition—maybe even to the NBA. Here's what happened: Some kids cooperated with my coaching effort and others didn't. At the end of the season, some of the most talented kids on the team were no different than when they started, while others had developed tremendously as players.

This is the nature of the work of the Holy Spirit. He wants to coach you. That's why the Bible says in 1 Thessalonians 5:19, "Do not hold back the work of the Holy Spirit" (NCV). And in Ephesians the Bible says, "Let the [Holy] Spirit change your way of thinking and make you into a new person" (4:23–24 CEV). Circle that word *let!* One of the wonders of the Christian life is that the Holy Spirit actually takes up residence inside of you. He enters into your inner world, your moral conscience, and your spirit. That's why Scripture says in Galatians 5, "Let us follow the Spirit's leading in every part of our lives" (v. 25 NLT). God wants to transform you. He wants you to come to him as you are; receive his gifts of grace, forgiveness, and love; and then let him begin the process of molding you and developing you into all that you were created to be and do. He'll use everything from prayer to relationships, from the Bible to key events. Make no mistake—you will be actively and supernaturally coached.

But our metaphor breaks down if we make it nothing more than coaching, because God will simultaneously do a work of creation in your life as you cooperate. Our life in Christ is something that is given and developed through our relationship with him. We must never reduce our spiritual life to something we develop on our own—it is the work of God in us.

Investment

This brings up the second way we enter into training: *investment.* You have to take the coaching you receive and the creative work God wants to perform and make the kind of investments necessary for that creative work to reach its maximum potential. Think of a mutual fund. You open the fund with an initial investment, say $1,000. If that is all you ever invest, then the amount of growth in your mutual fund will be very minimal and very slow. You must make continued investments for the fund to move forward and begin to generate the kind of dividends and growth you desire. Or more to the point, think of a new relationship. Say you meet someone at a party and have instant chemistry and many shared interests. But if you never connect with that person again, or at best, do so sparingly, then the hope of that relationship will never reach its potential.

You can become a Christian and never become a disciple. You can begin a life in Christ and then never develop it. "Most of us turned to Christ when we realized there was a difference between Christianity as a religion and Christianity as a relationship," writes Ken Gire. "Sometime after entering into that relationship with Christ, we realized something else. That there is a difference between a personal relationship with Christ and an intimate one."[17] You must cooperate with God's leading and direction in your life and make the necessary investments to position yourself for his ongoing work in your life. While living life spiritually consists of being, not doing, there are things you can *do* that will help you *be*! The goal of this book is to help you explore those "doings" for the sake of your being, beginning with God's manual for spiritual living—the Bible.

REFLECTION QUESTIONS

1. Do you truly see yourself as a son or daughter of God? How about as a saint?
2. With which deception of spirituality do you most identify?
3. Which myth did you most believe?

4. How susceptible are you to tackling the Christ life alone?

5. Have you fallen into the trap of thinking that discipleship is something you receive?

6. In what areas do you need to cooperate more with the work of the Holy Spirit? Where do you need to make more of an investment in your relationship with God?

CHAPTER TWO

HOW TO BIBLE

*Esteem this book as the precious fountain that
can never be exhausted.* —Martin Luther[1]

Google receives more than 63,000 searches per second on any given day, which translates into 3.8 million searches per minute, 228 million searches per hour, 5.6 billion searches per day, and at least 2 trillion searches per year.[2]

So where do we start when it comes to living the Christ life? Many people may google "how to Bible." At the time of this writing that search yielded 690 million results. Since we can't be sure how many of these are theologically sound, let me try to walk you through a few suggestions for "how to Bible."

A Quick Orientation

If you get hired for a job, you'll typically have to go through an orientation program. If you enroll in a college, you'll be required to go to a freshman orientation. Let's go through an orientation on the Bible in case you've never tried to dig into it before, or it didn't go very well when you did try.

As I wrote in *Christianity for People Who Aren't Christians*, there are four big headlines about the Bible.[3]

It's a Library

First, the Bible isn't a single book: it's a library, a collection of books. Sixty-six, to be exact, written by more than forty authors and covering a period of approximately fifteen hundred years.

Most of the books bear the name of the author. So the book of Isaiah is the book written by Isaiah. The book of Daniel is the book written by Daniel. Sometimes the books carry the name of the main event that the book discusses. For example, the book of Genesis is about the *genesis*—the creation, the beginning—of the world. The book of Exodus deals mostly with the great *exodus*, or departure, of the Jewish people from slavery under the leadership of Moses. A lot of the books are actually letters and carry the name of the people they were sent to. Philippians, for example, is the name of the book, or letter, sent to the people who lived in the city of Philippi. First and Second Corinthians are two letters sent to the people who lived in Corinth. First and Second Timothy are two letters a man named Paul sent to a man he was mentoring named Timothy. So the Bible is a library of books, reflecting different times in history, different authors, different settings, and different emphases.

It Has Two Testaments

The second big headline is that this library of books falls into two parts, usually called "testaments"—the Old Testament and the New Testament. The Old Testament is made up of thirty-nine of the sixty-six books, and the New Testament is made up of the remaining twenty-seven books.

The word *testament* simply means "agreement" or "covenant." It refers to a pact, a treaty, an alliance, an agreement between two parties. That tells you something about the content of the Bible. The Bible is a record of God's great covenants, his promises, with us in regard to our relationship with him. It's a record of God's dealings with us. The Old Testament is a record of God's agreements with people before the time of Jesus. The New Testament is a record of what transpired when Jesus came and following his resurrection.

So if you want to know what divides the Bible into the Old Testament and the New Testament, it is Jesus. He is the one who separates the two sections of Scripture. Jesus's coming altered all of history, and we designate all of sacred Scripture as being before Christ or after Christ. The Old Testament builds toward the New Testament; it looks forward to the New Testament. And then the New Testament fulfills the Old Testament and completes it, writing the final chapters to the story.

If you like the *Lord of the Rings* trilogy, you can think of the Old Testament as *The Fellowship of the Ring* followed by *The Two Towers* (the Old Testament takes two films because it has the most books) and then the New Testament is like the final installment, *The Return of the King*. If you don't like *The Lord of the Rings*, forget I said any of that. But like *The Lord of the Rings*, everything in the Bible *is* about the King.

Only his name is Jesus, not Aragorn.

So while the Bible is sixty-six books, in two parts, it's still one story. That's why it's called the Bible. The English word *Bible* comes from the name of the papyrus, or "byblos" reed, that was used for making scrolls and books. Because they were made from byblos reeds, books came to be known as bibles. But the writings of the Old Testament and the New Testament were so sacred, so special, so revered, that they came to be known simply as *the* book, or *the* Bible.

It's Sacred

But why are these books considered the sacred writings: Why these sixty-six books and not others? Why are these considered the Word of God? That's our third headline. Christians take the writings of the Bible as the Word of God for our lives for one reason: Jesus. Yes, the Old Testament was seen as sacred before Jesus—those books recorded God's dealings and God's prophets, who people saw and heard. But Jesus is the one who confirmed the Old Testament Scriptures as sacred and equally gave credence to the New Testament. If you believe Jesus was who he said he was— God himself in human form—then what he said is what matters more than anything. So if he said something was Scripture, or he set in motion the writing of something to be Scripture, then it *is* Scripture. If he was who he said he was, then it's not about what books I think ought to be set apart as sacred or inspired, or what books you think should make the cut, but what he said about it. And the Bible we have is the one he set apart.

Let's walk through that a bit. First, we accept the Old Testament as Scripture because Jesus did. When Jesus made reference to the Scriptures, he was referring to the Old Testament we have today. When the New Testament records Jesus saying he believed in the Scriptures, that meant the Old Testament because the New Testament had not been written yet. And here was his unqualified endorsement: "Truly I tell you, until heaven and earth disappear, not the smallest letter, not the least stroke of a pen, will by any means disappear from the Law [of Moses] until everything is accomplished" (Matt. 5:18). And then he also said, "[The] Scripture cannot be set aside" (John 10:35). In what may be one of the most intriguing statements he made in relation to the Old Testament, Jesus introduced a quote from the Old Testament by saying, "David himself, *speaking by the Holy Spirit*, declared . . ." (Mark 12:36, emphasis mine), and then went on to quote what David said in the Old Testament book of Psalms. Clearly, to Jesus, the Old Testament was no ordinary collection of writings. He referred to the writers of the Old Testament as being inspired by the Holy Spirit, thus giving us the very Word of God.

When we come to the New Testament, again, we look to Jesus to give it authority. First, because much of the New Testament records what he taught. If he was God in human form and taught something, it's safe to say the capturing of that teaching falls soundly under the category of sacred writings. He also laid the foundation for the writings of the rest of the New Testament to be accepted as Scripture through the apostles.

This is very important, and something a lot of Christians miss. Jesus chose the word *apostle* for a very small, select group of his disciples in order to indicate their unique role. The word *apostle* means "those who have been sent," and the mission Jesus sent them on was that of preaching and teaching. The word is used only of the twelve originally chosen by Jesus and a handful of select others, most notably the apostle Paul. The apostles received a unique commission from Jesus himself—never to be repeated—to assume a prophetic role and speak God's word to the people. These were the men who were to speak in Jesus's name and carry his word to others. They carried the very authority of Jesus himself as they taught. Jesus even said these words to them, as recorded in the New Testament book of Matthew: "Anyone who welcomes you, welcomes me" (10:40).

Each apostle was given a personal commission by Jesus himself—they were *never* self-appointed. The most literal translation of the Greek language has Jesus saying to Paul in Acts 26:16, "I apostle you." Each was then given a historical experience of interaction with Jesus himself. They spent time with Jesus and were mentored by Jesus. This is why when a replacement was selected for Judas, the principle requirement was that the person be someone who had been with Jesus throughout his ministry so they could be a true eyewitness and direct bearer of the teaching of Jesus. For Paul, the last apostle appointed, it was a post-resurrection interaction and appointment. Without this, he could not have been an apostle.

> **▶ FOUR BIG HEADLINES**
>
> IT'S A LIBRARY
> IT HAS TWO TESTAMENTS
> IT'S SACRED
> IT'S INSPIRED

Each apostle was given a special inspiration for their teaching from Jesus himself through the Holy Spirit. While all Christians have the Holy Spirit within them from the moment of conversion, Jesus promised the apostles a special ministry of the Holy Spirit in regard to their teaching and writing. The Holy Spirit gave them a remembrance of the teaching of Jesus and inspired them to teach other truths from God as well. Jesus also said that they would be guided into all truth: "The Spirit shows what is true and will come and guide you into the full truth . . . by taking my message and telling it to you" (John 16:13–14 CEV). This is why the teachings of the apostles were considered Scripture, and the mark of what would be included in the New Testament was simple: Was it written by, or based on, the teaching of Jesus or one of his apostles? This is also why we read in the second chapter of Acts, which records the history of the early church, these words: "[The early church] *devoted themselves to the apostles' teaching*" (v. 42, emphasis mine). The early church knew who the apostles were in the grander scheme of things—they had heard Jesus appoint them! They saw and heard Jesus teach about what kind of role the apostles were going to have. They knew that Peter and John, James and Paul, in this sense, were not ordinary men. The teaching of the apostles was the teaching of Christ. To receive them was to receive Christ; to reject them was to reject Christ.

So, when it comes to the Bible, we didn't choose these books. They aren't something a group of church leaders sat down one day and randomly picked. Jesus had already embraced and affirmed the Old Testament as the Word of God; the first four books of the New Testament capture his own life and teaching as God himself in human form come to earth; the rest of the New Testament was personally commissioned by Jesus and written by his handpicked apostles, through a special working of the Holy Spirit as they wrote.

This means that what we have in the Bible is God's revelation to us. The word *revelation* comes from the Latin word *revelatio* that means to "draw back the curtain." It is a theatrical term. Imagine a stage where a play is about to begin. You can't know the story until the curtain is pulled back, until it's "revealed." That's the Bible—God's *revelation*. It's God revealing himself and truth about himself that could not otherwise be known.

It's Inspired

This brings us to our fourth and final headline. The Bible isn't a normal book. It's inspired by God, and we shouldn't water that word down. Sometimes we use the word *inspired* to mean that something was wonderfully creative, such as a painting by Rembrandt, or music by Bach, or a play by Shakespeare. Sometimes we use the word to refer to something that we feel—how we find a beautiful sunset or a powerful speech to be inspiring.

You need to get that out of your head. Inspiration, as it relates to the Bible, is much more profound. When Paul was describing it in his second letter to Timothy, he put it this way:

> But you must remain faithful to the things you have been taught. You know they are true, for you know you can trust those who taught you. You have been taught the holy Scriptures from childhood, and they have given you the wisdom to receive the salvation that comes by trusting in Christ Jesus. All Scripture is inspired by God and is useful to teach us what is true and to make us realize what is wrong in our lives. It corrects us when we are wrong and teaches us to do what is right. God uses it to prepare and equip his people to do every good work. (2 Tim. 3:14–17 NLT)

The Greek word Paul used for *inspired* literally meant "God-breathed." That's the idea behind the inspiration of the Scriptures. Breathed out by God, exhaled by God, produced by God. *It's not a human book*. It was written by humans, but as they were moved by God. It reflects their personality, vocabulary, and writing style, but the act of writing itself was stirred by God. More than three thousand times in the Bible we find the writers using some form of the expression, "The Lord says." The prophet Jeremiah recorded God saying to him, "I [God] have put my words in your mouth" (Jer. 1:9). The idea of inspiration is that God used people to write the books of the Bible but was so involved in the process that they wrote exactly what he wanted. One of the clearest expressions of this idea was given by the apostle Peter: "Above all, you must realize that no prophecy in Scripture ever came from the prophet's own understanding, or from human initiative. No, those prophets were moved by the Holy Spirit, and they spoke from God" (2 Pet. 1:20–21 NLT).

How to Read It

Jesus was once asked a number of questions by a group of spiritual explorers. He answered each one of them patiently, but finally, after the questions kept coming and coming, he turned around and asked them something interesting. He asked, "You do not know the Scriptures. . . . Have you not read what God said to you?" (Matt. 22:29, 31). Jesus was surprised that people who claimed to be interested in spiritual things had never bothered to read the primary text.

You must not make that mistake.

But how do you read the Bible?

Get a Contemporary Translation

First, get a contemporary translation to read. Many people who have tried to read the Bible have found it difficult to read, and there was a reason—it was! And the reason it was is because they tried to read it in an outdated translation that almost doomed them to failure.

The Bible was basically written in two languages: Hebrew and Greek. The Old Testament was written in the language of its writers—Hebrew—and the New Testament was written in the most-used language of its day—Greek. That means all of our Bibles today are translations of those original languages. That's why scholars who do such translating—usually large teams of academics—study Hebrew and Greek. Of course, the Bible is not alone in this—translations are necessary for every ancient manuscript. Whatever language a manuscript was originally written in—Greek, Hebrew, Latin, French, Russian, or German—if you read it in English, it's a translation. So get a Bible that has been translated into English. And not just English, but the way we use the English language today. That's why there are so many translations out there. It's not because we don't know what the original Hebrew and Greek manuscripts contain—it's because the English language changes so much. When the Bible was translated in the 1600s, the Greek and Hebrew manuscripts were translated into the language of that day, which was King James English. You may have heard of the King James Bible. It was commissioned by King James and therefore was written in King James English, meaning that there were lots of *thee*s, *thou*s, *heretofore*s, and other words we either don't use today or that don't make sense today because we use them differently. Some examples of more modern translations that I would recommend reading include the New International Version and the New Living Translation.

Start with Jesus

Now, where to start? You're probably thinking, *Well, at the beginning.* Actually, I wouldn't recommend that. Since the Bible is a library of books, you don't have to start with Genesis and work your way through. In fact, that's probably not the best way to get into it. I'd start with Jesus. He's the heart of it all. This means starting off with one of the four biographies of his life—the New Testament books of Matthew, Mark, Luke, and John, named after the men who wrote them.

Each biography tells the story a little differently, because of the authors' own personalities and who they were trying to convey the story of Jesus to. Matthew was written to the Jews of his day. Mark was the youngest of the four biographers, and his biography is the shortest and is filled with the most action scenes. Luke was the scholar of the group and is commonly ranked as a first-class historian because of his eye for detail. John's was the last one to be written. He had a wider, more secular, Greek audience in mind. And as the last that was written, John intentionally included many details about the life of Jesus that the first three left out.

I usually recommend starting with John. After that, read another New Testament book, like James, which is a brief letter to some of the early church communities that will give you a taste of the Bible's practical advice on how to live the life of a Christ follower. Then I'd go back and read the first book, Genesis. After you've read those three books—John, James, and Genesis—you're probably in good shape to jump in wherever you want and your interest leads.

Learn How to Interpret What You Read

But how do you interpret what you read? Isn't that where it gets sticky? Not really. Just read it with a normal eye toward discovery. Did you ever take a journalism class? Here are the questions every reporter is trained to ask: *Who? What? Where? When? Why? How?*

Ask that of the Bible!

Ask questions like, *Who is speaking? Who was it written to? What are the main ideas?* And then, once you've asked those, dig in deeper, asking things like this:

What was the background of the writer?

What was going on at that time in history?

What seems to be the key section or verse in the passage?

Then, once you've done that, you can interpret what you've read with the basic principles of interpretation. And there are three main principles: First, always try to find out what the author's intent was. If you want to know what a particular part of the Bible means, the primary goal is to find out what the writer wanted it to mean. Find out what it *originally* meant. This will also help in cutting through the various cultural issues that might have been at play in that day and time.

Second, always try to interpret the verse in light of its context. Taking a verse out of context is one of the most common mistakes people make with the Bible. Remember that a verse is part of a chapter, a chapter is part of a book, and a book is part of a library of books. Don't isolate a verse from its wider context. If you read something that makes you scratch your head, read everything the Bible says about it and let that complete the picture of the individual statement or teaching.

Of particular importance is to read the Old Testament in light of the New Testament. While the entire Bible is God's Word, equally inspired, it is a progressive revelation—meaning, an unfolding story culminating in Jesus and the church. Remember the Old Testament contains the covenants God made with men and women about how to be in relationship with him before Christ came. The New Testament is the new agreement God made with men and women about how to be in a relationship with God after the coming of Christ. But it didn't replace the old covenants—it fulfilled them. The older covenants contained pointers and signs of what was to come, all finding completion in the new covenant brought by Jesus.

All along God's intention was to bring forth the Savior of the world in the person of Jesus. The purpose of the old covenant, or what is often called the law, was to prepare the people for the coming, complete covenant that would arrive with the Messiah. Here's the principle: all of the Old Testament applies to Christians, but none of it applies apart from its fulfillment in Christ. The law of the Old Testament provides us with a paradigm of timeless ethical, moral, and theological principles. But some laws no longer have validity because they have been completely fulfilled in Christ, such as the sacrificial system. So we obey the laws of sacrifice by trusting in Christ as our once-for-all sacrifice, not by bringing sheep or goats to be slaughtered. The kosher laws were designed to set the Israelites apart from the other nations, so we obey these laws when we morally separate ourselves from sin.[4]

Think of something as basic as the Old Testament telling us an "eye for an eye" and the New Testament commanding us to "turn the other cheek." Contradiction? No. It's a fulfillment issue. The "eye for an eye" passage in Exodus 21 was all about whether you could pursue private vendettas and retaliate when you had been wronged. The answer was "no." That was for the judges to decide. Instead, they were to follow a principle based on "an eye for an eye," meaning compensation and restitution in direct proportion to the crime. They were to match the damages inflicted—and no more. You were not to have blood feuds or private wars. So "an eye for an eye" was a literary device to give a formula for compensation.

Then Jesus gave its fulfillment:

> You have heard the law that says the punishment must match the injury: "An eye for an eye, and a tooth for a tooth." But I say, do not resist an evil person! If someone slaps you on the right cheek, offer the other cheek also. If you are sued in court and your shirt is taken from you, give your coat too. If a soldier demands that you carry his gear for a mile, carry it two miles. Give to those who ask, and don't turn away from those who want to borrow. (Matt. 5:38–42 NLT)

Do you hear what he's saying? "You have heard of 'an eye for an eye'—and that's good—but I tell you to go farther! Don't retaliate at all! Don't harbor a spirit of resentment. If someone does you wrong, meet it by doing them something right!" That type of fulfillment ran throughout Jesus's teaching and throughout the New Testament. Over and over the letter of the law was met with the greater, more challenging *spirit* of the law. Jesus would say, "You have heard you are not to commit adultery—but I tell you, don't lust in your heart!" "You've heard not to commit murder—I tell you, don't hate!" (See Jesus's Sermon on the Mount found in Matthew 5.) Jesus wanted to take the law and put it in people's hearts.

The final principle is to always let Scripture interpret Scripture. If you want to know what a particular verse or chapter might be trying to say about marriage or parenting or money or sex, the best way to be sure you're getting it right is to make sure that it lines up with everything else the Bible says about that subject.

Of course the biggest interpretation issues often lie with the questions that start with, "Is it okay for a Christian to . . . ?" Guidance on how they should live is probably one of the biggest things people are looking for when they read the Bible. When you find yourself asking "Is it okay for a Christian to . . . ?" consider it in light of this little diagram:

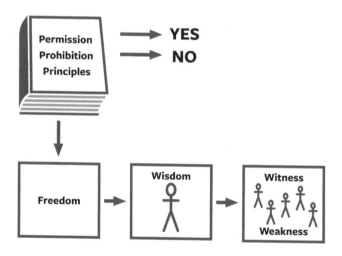

Think of it as a four-stage process. First, with every issue, we want to go to the Bible and see what it has to say. And when we do, we'll find out that we're either given clear permission, a firm prohibition, or a set of relevant principles to navigate the issue.

What we won't find is silence. There may be a firm "no." There may be a firm "yes." Or there may be ideas and principles that inform our decision making.

If the Bible gives a clear denunciation and warning about any involvement with something—in other words, you check with the Bible on whether something is okay, and the answer is clearly "no"—then you can stop. You have your answer. The same, obviously, with a clear affirmation. But what if the Bible doesn't give a ready-made answer lying on the surface of things? Instead of a permission, or blanket prohibition, it often gives freedom within the limits of a set of principles and boundaries.

That is what will lead us to step two, which is taking the Bible's permissions and principles and relating them to the freedom we have in Christ. Not just freedom unchecked, but freedom informed by the Bible's principles and boundaries, wisdom and counsel. Once we've explored the freedom we have in Christ for our life, in light of all the Bible has to say, we take the next step. This is how it all should best play out in our own life.

It's not enough to find out what the Bible says about where we have freedom and where we don't, or even what boundaries and principles should be followed in pursuit of that freedom. The third step is thinking about yourself in relation to the freedom and the Bible's principles. Every single one of us is unique. We have a temperament, a nature, a life situation, a history. There are areas where we are weak and where we are strong. Biblically, you may find that there's an area where you have the freedom to do something, but it still isn't wise for you to do it. It might not be foolish for others, but it would be foolish for you. This is why when we come to the third box, the big issue is about wisdom, asking, "What is the wisest thing for *me* to do?" Again, the answer may be very different for others than for you.

The fourth stage has to do with our responsibility as Christ followers before a watching world. There are people watching us. We are interacting with people in the context of community. We have a responsibility as Christ followers in terms of how our behavior might be perceived. There may be something that a Christ follower has absolute freedom to do—and there is nothing in their life that would warn them away from it—but if that freedom is not exercised with discretion, it could be damaging to those around them who will interpret the freedom as disavowing Christ. This is how the apostle Paul wrote about it: "You say, 'I am allowed to do anything'—but not everything is good for you. You say, 'I am allowed to do anything'—but not everything is beneficial. Don't be concerned for your own good but for the good of others" (1 Cor. 10:23–24 NLT).

In Paul's case, the issue was whether to eat meat that had previously been sacrificed to idols. He affirmed that Christians had the freedom to eat whatever they wanted, but if they were in a situation where eating said meat would signal that they too were eating it in worship to that idol, they should refrain. The context and public perception were everything. So this isn't about offending another Christ follower who doesn't want you exercising a particular freedom. It's not about following a false moral code that is a caricature of Christian morality that, in truth, doesn't matter to a nonbeliever's assessment of the nature or object of your faith. If you're free in Christ, you're free in Christ, whether they want you to be or not. No, this is about handling that freedom in a way that would cause someone who is not a Christ follower to wonder whether there is integrity in who you say you follow.

Read with a Heart for Reflection

Finally, and most important of all, read the Bible with a heart for reflection. The Hebrew word for *meditate* means "to mutter or to mumble, to make a low sound." It was the habit of people reflecting on the Scriptures to turn the words and meanings over and over in their minds, and they did this by repeating the words to themselves, often in a whisper that sounded very much like mumbling. The point is not to verbally repeat the words you study aloud, but to so reflect upon them that they penetrate into the depths of your heart.[5]

I am reminded of an old story of a very learned man who came to visit a rabbi. The scholar was close to thirty, but he had never before visited a rabbi.

"What have you done all your life?" the rabbi asked him.

"I have gone through the whole of the Talmud three times," answered the learned man.

"Yes, but how much of the Talmud has gone through you?" the rabbi inquired.[6]

That is the key to all Bible reading. Not how many times you've gone through the Bible, but how many times the Bible has gone through you.

Following Through

The truth is that the Bible is not difficult to read nor difficult to understand. It's difficult to follow through on what it says because in so many ways we resist its leadership. So, if I may be so bold, here are a few "natural" ways any one of us may try to circumvent its very clear teaching.

The Cosmic Exception Clause

The first game we play is what I call the "cosmic exception clause." Most of us are familiar with exception clauses. This is when there's an exception, an escape, a way out from under a clear command or prohibition—a time or place or situation when it doesn't apply. Some people want to have exception clauses with the Bible. They know what it means to apply what the Bible says to a particular area of their life—sexually, financially, relationally— but they think to themselves, *In my case, and in my situation, it doesn't apply. I'm unique. I'm different. My circumstances allow me to bypass this one.*

That's the cosmic exception clause. That somehow, someway, you don't have to apply what the Bible says to your life the way it says you should. You're the exception, so you give yourself a kitchen pass. But what you're doing is placing yourself above God. Your own word about your life, your own assessment of what's best, trumps God's. Which not only makes the Bible meaningless and impotent in your life—guaranteeing that you will never grow spiritually or become who God dreams of you becoming—but it also separates you, relationally, from God. Consider these words from the apostle John: "If someone claims, 'I know God,' but doesn't obey God's commandments, that person is a liar and is not living in the truth. But those who obey God's word truly show how completely they love him. That is how we know we are living in him. Those who say they live in God should live their lives as Jesus did" (1 John 2:4–6 NLT).

> *What matters is not how many times you've gone through the Bible, but how many times the Bible has gone through you.*

The Food Bar

A second way we can avoid applying the Bible to our life is more subtle than the cosmic exception clause. Let's call it the food bar approach. You grab your tray, and you start down the line. Some things you like and some things you don't. So what will end up on your plate—things you hate? Not likely. It's piled high with stuff that goes down easy. Comfort food. But since you're eating, since you have actual food on your tray, you tell yourself that you're doing fine.

See how subtle it is?

I recently read an article that detailed how restaurants that offer "all-you-can-eat" buffets work to ensure that people don't necessarily get the best food but fill up fast and move on. They put the cheap, filling food at the front of the buffet line, because 75 percent of buffet customers select whatever food is in the first tray. They use smaller plates. They use larger than average serving spoons for cheaper foods, like potatoes, and smaller than average tongs for costlier meats. The waitstaff works hard to keep water glasses filled, using extra-large glasses.[7] While restaurants may manipulate us along these lines, we shouldn't be doing it to ourselves. If you treat the Bible this way, you will end up with some comfortable insights and principles on things like marriage and parenting, but pass up the uncomfortable, lifestyle-changing applications on money and sex. At the end you walk away with only the areas of God's leadership in your life that you like. The ones that taste good. The ones that don't challenge how you're living or need to live.

This is not applying the Bible to your life. When you approach the Bible like a food bar, you're the one in charge. You assign God a place in your back pocket where you can whip him out whenever it's comfortable and put him away whenever it's not.

The Great Compromise

One more game we can play is the compromise game, and this one may be the darkest of all. We play the compromise game and water down the clear teaching of the Bible by denying it actually says what it says, or we water down its authority by convincing ourselves that what it says is just wrong. Why? Because we don't like what it says.

In truth, we're just demonstrating raw, willful rebellion. We try to get away from applying the Bible to our life because we don't want to surrender our life. We don't want to give our money. We don't want to move out. We don't want to stop sleeping around. We don't want to repair that relationship. The Bible confronts our life at the deepest, most uncomfortable, most life-changing levels imaginable. And we either welcome the confrontation or fight it. We either let God's Word transform us or we let it threaten us. Let's be clear—the Bible is not tame. It is God's Word. As the Bible itself says, "For the word of God is alive and powerful. It is sharper than the sharpest two-edged sword, cutting between soul and spirit, between joint and marrow. It exposes our innermost thoughts and desires. Nothing in all creation is hidden from God. Everything is naked and exposed before his eyes, and he is the one to whom we are accountable" (Heb. 4:12–13 NLT).

This means you can read the Bible one of two ways. You can read it with a surrendered heart where with every page you ask yourself, "What attitude do I need to change? What do I need to start doing or stop doing? What things do I need to stop believing or start believing? What relationships do I need to work on? What ministry should I be having with others?"[8]

Or you can read it with a defensive, rebellious spirit that fights its work in your life. It's your call. But only one will give you the life in Christ you long for.

Missing Jesus

Early in his life, Billy Graham wrestled with whether he was going to embrace the Bible as the inspired, revealed Word of God and therefore the ultimate truth-source for his life, or view it through eyes that dismissed it as a fallible, unreliable book of merely human insight. He intuitively knew that this was no mere intellectual decision, but that it would alter the very trajectory of his life.

He had a friend named Chuck Templeton who, at the time, was facing the same decision. Both were rising stars in the evangelical world, although most considered Templeton the better speaker of the two. But as Templeton looked at the Bible, he made the conscious decision not to believe it and to view it as little more than any other book. He then went to work on Graham to take a similar position.

The resolution for Graham came while he was at a student conference at Forest Home, a retreat center in the San Bernardino Mountains near Los Angeles. Graham went for a walk in the surrounding pine forest. About fifty yards off the main trail, he sat for a long time on a large rock that was there, with his Bible spread open on a tree stump. Then he made his choice, ultimately and finally, praying, "Oh God, I cannot prove certain things. I cannot answer some of the questions Chuck is raising and some of the other people are raising, but I accept this Book by faith as the Word of God."[9]

And that, Graham would later say, changed everything.

I've been to Forest Home and, on a similar walk, I accidentally stumbled on the very rock where Graham made his lifelong values choice. I knew it was the same rock, because there is now a bronze tablet on the stone, commemorating his decision. Why such recognition? Because it was through that decision that Graham was able to be used by God to change the world. Here's how Graham himself reflected on it:

> [That single resolution] gave power and authority to my preaching that has never left me. The gospel in my hands became a hammer and a flame. . . . I felt as though I had a rapier in my hands and through the power of the Bible was slashing deeply into men's consciousness, leading them to surrender to God.[10]

Sadly, the world never heard any more from Chuck Templeton. He ended up resigning from the ministry and eventually left the faith altogether. He was interviewed at the age of eighty-three, while he was living with Alzheimer's disease. Asked by a journalist about his youthful decision, he reflected back on his life and said that he missed Jesus. And then he broke down in tears and could say no more.

REFLECTION QUESTIONS

1. What's most significant to you about the fact that the Bible was inspired by God and not just written by human beings?

2. The Bible is a timeless book, in that God covered topics that are still important to us today, like work, marriage, family, relationships, finances, stress, love, health, and time. Which areas of life are you most thankful that God's Word covers?

3. It's so easy to divide life into separate categories (work, family, exercise, spirituality, etc.). Why is it important to avoid keeping spirituality in a separate box off to the side?

4. After we read the Bible, it's important to believe it and follow it. Why is that often difficult?

5. Have you been playing games with the Bible, picking and choosing to follow only what you like?

CHAPTER THREE

TALKING TO GOD

The New Testament contains embarrassing promises that what we pray for with faith we shall receive. —C. S. Lewis[1]

There is a spiritual act that almost every single person on the planet, in one form or another, has done. No matter where they stand with God, Jesus, the Bible, religion, faith—it doesn't matter. It's an almost universal act at one point or another.

We've prayed.

It may have been short, it may have been prayed in crisis mode or out of fear, it may have even been prayed in hope . . . but we've all done it. But do we know what we're doing when we do it? A lot of us don't. It's not like there is an official school on how to pray.

But there was an official teacher.

When Jesus taught on how to pray, he didn't say anything about a particular place you had to go to pray. He didn't say anything at all about a specific day or time. He didn't say anything about how you should dress. He didn't say anything about whether you should stand or sit, kneel or lie down. He never mentioned whether you should close your eyes or talk in your head or out loud.

So what did he say?

When you pray, don't babble on and on as the Gentiles do. They think their prayers are answered merely by repeating their words again and again. Don't be like them, for your Father knows exactly what you need even before you ask him! Pray like this:

Our Father in heaven,
    may your name be kept holy.
May your Kingdom come soon.
May your will be done on earth,
    as it is in heaven.
Give us today the food we need,
and forgive us our sins,
    as we have forgiven those who sin against us.
And don't let us yield to temptation,
    but rescue us from the evil one.

If you forgive those who sin against you, your heavenly Father will forgive you. But if you refuse to forgive others, your Father will not forgive your sins. (Matt. 6:7–15 NLT)

That prayer, in its various forms as we've continued to translate the original Greek manuscripts and Aramaic words into contemporary English, is often called the Lord's Prayer. And it does need to be contemporized because we don't use words like *art* or *hallowed* (as in "Our Father Who art in heaven, hallowed be Thy name") anymore. It's good that we keep translating it into more current language, because Jesus never meant it to be a formula. He never meant it to be something we repeat, word for word, like a magical spell. He even starts off instructing us not to babble or repeat words over and over again. That's not what prayer is meant to entail.

What Jesus gives us in that passage is a guideline. He is saying, "Pray like this . . . Here's how it should feel . . . Pray along these lines . . . Make it something like this . . ." In his model, we find seven very specific, very practical insights into how to pray.

Intimate

First, Jesus shows us that when we talk to God in prayer, we should be intimate. How do we know that? Because Jesus started his example on how to pray by saying, "Pray like this: Our Father . . ."

(Matt. 6:9 NLT). As we learned in the opening pages of this book, he actually used the Aramaic word *Abba*. He said, "I want you to pray this way. I want you to begin by saying, 'Our Abba in Heaven . . .'" Again, *Abba* was the most intimate family term there was, used between a very small child and their parent.[2]

When a child talks to a parent in a healthy parent-child relationship, there is disarming honesty, an absence of guile, utter transparency, boundless affection, unquenchable curiosity, and absolute truth.

My grandchildren call me Papa. They don't call me Dr. White or Sir. I can't imagine them coming to me, standing at attention, saluting, and saying, "Oh glorious potentate, founder of our family, might I crawleth on thy lap in order to snuggle?"[3] No, it's Papa. And I want to always be Papa. Just like I still love hearing my very adult kids call me Daddy. Jesus said we should pray to God like that because God loves it too. That's how he feels toward us and wants us to feel toward him. So pray that way. Like a child to their father. Not childish in the sense of immaturity or in the sense of meaningless chatter, but childlike in the sense of the relationship itself. When a child talks to a parent in a healthy parent-child relationship, there is disarming honesty, an absence of guile, utter transparency, boundless affection, unquenchable curiosity, and absolute truth.

In other words, true intimacy.

This is exactly what God wants from us.

Expectant

Jesus also lets us know that when we talk to God in prayer we should be expectant. We should pray as if we expect it to matter—expect God to be able to respond and in ways only God can. Did you notice what Jesus said in our passage? When we call out to God, it isn't just to our Abba, but our Abba *in heaven*. We pray to the Abba who is all powerful, all knowing, and ever present. This means that when we pray, we should pray with a sense of expectation, knowing that we're praying to the God in heaven.

The God who can act.

The God who can intervene.

The God who can make a difference.

This raises one of the biggest questions people ask about prayer: Why should I pray when God already *knows* that I'm thankful or that I need help? The answer is that prayer is not simply communication, it is a *relational* event. It's not just the transmission of information—it's a time when you as a child go to your Father in heaven and spend time talking to him. Also, the Bible clearly teaches that God has chosen to act in response to our prayers. He has chosen to invest his power, to channel his strength, in direct relation to people communicating with him. If you find yourself thinking, *Why should I pray? God is going to do what God is going to do*, remember that what God has said he will do is to take our prayers into account. Prayer does not *control* God, but he has said that when we pray, we invite his active participation into our lives in the way he has asked to be invited.

> *Prayer does not control God, but he has said that when we pray, we invite his active participation into our lives.*

As you are reading this, I would be willing to bet that you have something weighing on you right now. You might be going through a very difficult time in your life. You might be experiencing stress, worry, even fear. You may be facing a critical decision or considering what could only be called a leap of faith. Are you praying as if to the God in heaven? Are you praying as if to the God who can act?

This is why it is so senseless not to pray. It betrays a functional atheism, as if you either do not believe in God or you do not believe

God has the power to act and to make a difference. The fact is that God can do anything, and he's just waiting for us to recognize his power and ask for his help. One of the healthiest things that you can do when you're praying is to remind yourself that you are praying to the God who has done every single miracle in all of human history. Every single unbelievable, jaw-dropping story you have ever read or heard about in the Bible—you're praying to that God. And he's listening to you! Just as he listened to Abraham, Isaac, Jacob, Joseph, Moses, David, Joshua, Elijah, Elisha, . . . Jesus! You are praying to the God who can act. Why wouldn't you offer your prayers up to him?

Reverent

Next, Jesus said that when we pray, it should be appropriately reverent, done in a way that God's "name be kept holy" (Matt. 6:9 NLT). The name of God represents God himself—his very nature and being. So when we pray, God should be honored, lifted up, held in high regard . . . *respected*. This means our prayers should be intimate, but never cavalier. They should be honest, but never trite. They should be natural, but never careless or nonchalant.

In the Bible, there is a powerful scene where the prophet Isaiah comes into the presence of God. The description he offers is telling:

> I saw the Lord, high and exalted, seated on a throne; and the train of his robe filled the temple. Above him were seraphim, each with six wings: With two wings they covered their faces, with two they covered their feet, and with two they were flying. And they were calling to one another:
>
> > "Holy, holy, holy is the LORD Almighty;
> > the whole earth is full of his glory."
>
> At the sound of their voices the doorposts and thresholds shook and the temple was filled with smoke. (Isa. 6:1–4)

That's not a God to be trifled with. What Jesus is after is for us to never forget that God is God and to interact with him accordingly. Not in fear, but very much in honor. So when we pray, it should be real but reverent.

Submitted

One of the fastest-growing sports is MMA (mixed martial arts). When there is submission in an MMA fight, it means one of the fighters yields to their opponent. They can "tap out" with their hand or foot, hitting the floor to signal they're done. The next dynamic when it comes to prayer is that we should begin by "tapping out"—meaning, when we pray we should be submitted. In other words, we should pray along these lines: "May your Kingdom come soon. May your will be done on earth, as it is in heaven" (Matt. 6:10 NLT).

Prayer isn't just about you talking to God, but about God talking to you. It is about you searching out what it is God wants for your life, what he cares about, the agenda he wants you to have. The goal of prayer isn't that you bend God's will to yours, but to pray in such a way that you bend your will to his. To find out what he is doing, and then join him.

Perhaps you are like me when you pray. My first tendency is to ask God to do what I want him to do, or to show up and bless what I've already decided to do. That isn't what I should be doing. I should be asking for his guidance and direction; asking for him to let me know what I should do. But there's a bigger picture here than just our individual lives. To pray for God's will to come and his kingdom to take root is to pray for the entire *world* to "tap out" for God: to yield, to submit. To have the kingdom of heaven, which means heaven's values, heaven's standards, extend over the earth.

If I'm praying for God's will to come, his kingdom to come, I'm praying for just that—for it to *come*. In governments and institutions, businesses and the marketplace, the media, the judicial system, and education. I'm praying for the kingdom to come to bear on racism and sexism, human trafficking and poverty, homelessness and unemployment, orphans and widows, the sick and the hungry. And most of all, bringing it to bear on lives that are far from God, so that they can come near to God, come home, and have that relationship restored through Jesus—experiencing grace, forgiveness, a new beginning, and a new life. This means when the prayer ends and I get up off my knees, I'm becoming that agent of change. I'm the revolutionary. Praying is meant to have a dangerous edge, because when you pray the way Jesus tells you to, you can't help but become something of a radical in terms of how you go through life. Why? You're one of those helping to bring that kingdom into reality.

Dependent

So when we talk to God, we should be intimate, expectant, reverent, and submitted. We should also be dependent. Jesus said that when we pray, we should always remember to pray in a way that demonstrates our dependence on God, as in "Give us today the food we need" (Matt. 6:11 NLT). Isn't that as foundationally dependent as you can be? Asking for daily food? Yet the spirit of this aspect of prayer goes beyond food—this is about daily *everything*.

"God, give me today the insight and patience I need to raise my children.

"Give me today the sensitivity, commitment, and resolve I need for my marriage.

"Give me today the money I need, the job I need, the knowledge I need, the strength I need, the wisdom I need, the discernment I need."

Not in a spirit that demands, but a spirit that depends.

Honest

Then Jesus added these words: "And forgive us our sins, as we have forgiven those who sin against us" (Matt. 6:12 NLT). There are two aspects of forgiveness there, not one. We really like the first one and we really *don't* like the second. As has often been quipped, everyone thinks forgiveness is a wonderful idea until they have someone to forgive.

The heart of what Jesus is telling us is that when we talk to God in prayer, we should be honest and authentic. Being honest when we talk to God means that we don't try to play games with who we are, what we've done, or the choices we've made. God knows the sin in our life—he wants to see if we'll be authentic enough to own up to it in his presence when we converse with him. He wants to know whether we'll be honest enough to say, "Father, there are some ways that I have really screwed up. I've done some things, I've said some things, I've viewed some things, I've participated in some things that I know did not please you.

"I know I disappointed you. And I did it willfully and purposefully, and some of them I didn't even blush about at the time. I'm so sorry. And it's not just for things I've done, but things I've thought. Things I've felt. Things not just on the outside, but on the inside. My sin is not simply of the flesh, but of the spirit—pride, envy, hate. I so need to come clean with you about them. I want to own them and confess them to you—no games or excuses—and tell you how sorry I am and ask for your forgiveness."

When you do that, you're praying the way Jesus said you should. But there's a dynamic attached to this. When you drink deeply from the well of forgiveness, it should feed your own forgiving spirit toward

> **WHEN WE PRAY, WE SHOULD BE ...**
>
> INTIMATE
> EXPECTANT
> REVERENT
> SUBMITTED
> DEPENDENT
> HONEST
> HUMBLE

others. "If you forgive those who sin against you, your heavenly Father will forgive you. But if you refuse to forgive others, your Father will not forgive your sins" (Matt. 6:14–15 NLT). In other words, the reception of grace should lead to the extension of grace. To ask for forgiveness for your sin but to not give forgiveness for another's sin is spiritually unconscionable. It's simply too much of a spiritual disconnect to have your own request for forgiveness be acknowledged when you refuse it to another. But if you seek to forgive others, then that spiritual authenticity flows into your life along with God's radical forgiveness for your sin as well. Jesus made this point throughout his teaching, such as with the famed story of the unmerciful servant (Matt. 18:21–35).

This is immensely difficult, I know. That's why Jesus said to make the effort to forgive a matter of prayer. Literally asking God for help to forgive. You might be thinking, *You mean it's fair for me to say, God, can you help me forgive because I'm having a hard time with this?* Yes, that's part of being authentic and real in your prayers. Jesus was once asked about the number of times someone should be forgiven. Should it be seven? Jesus said, "No, seventy times seven!" (Matt. 18:22). The point wasn't to establish a ceiling of forgiving someone 490 times, and then you're done. The point was that forgiveness is never to end. Even when seventy times seven isn't for different people who have hurt you, but when you're asking seventy times seven for the same person for the same act. It may be a lifelong prayer to help you keep forgiving someone. Praying for forgiveness should never end, especially because your personal need for it for your own sins will never end.

Humble

Finally, Jesus offered this insight into how to pray: "And don't let us yield to temptation, but rescue us from the evil one" (Matt. 6:13 NLT). Some of you who might be familiar with the traditional King James English translation of the Lord's Prayer might be thinking, *I thought it was "deliver us from evil"?* Actually, when translating from the original Greek language, it specifically says "evil one." Which is why if there's a single word for this guideline, I would argue for the word *humble*.

The heart of humility is knowing exactly where you stand. It's being a realist. It's knowing your weaknesses and strengths. It's having a healthy sense of where and when you need help. When we pray, we should be under no illusions about the nature of what we're up against, and how completely unable we are to meet it on our own. Jesus makes it very clear: we *will* come up against temptation and the work of the evil one. Every day we will be tempted to do things that will embarrass God, to move away from him rather than closer to him. This means we are in desperate need of God's help to live the way we're supposed to live. Jesus said if you are going to pray in a way that is spiritually authentic, you will have the humility to pray that you will be delivered, be kept safe, from the evil one.

To be clear, yes, Jesus is talking about the person of the devil (or Satan). Sorry if that unnerves you a bit, but Jesus was very matter-of-fact about the reality of Satan. All of Scripture is matter-of-fact about his existence and presence and power. For example, take a look at how the Bible talks about this in the letter written to the Christ followers in the city of Ephesus:

> A final word: Be strong in the Lord and in his mighty power. Put on all of God's armor so that you will be able to stand firm against all strategies of the devil. For we are not fighting against flesh-and-blood enemies, but against evil rulers and authorities of the unseen world, against mighty powers in this dark world, and against evil spirits in the heavenly places. (Eph. 6:10–12 NLT)

Or as Eugene Peterson powerfully paraphrased it,

> This is no afternoon athletic contest that we'll walk away from and forget about in a couple of hours. This is for keeps, a life-or-death fight to the finish against the Devil and all his angels. (Eph. 6:12 MSG)

The idea of having spiritual humility when it comes to the evil one is all throughout the Bible. The early church leader Peter, one of the original disciples of Jesus, wrote: "So humble yourselves under the mighty power of God. . . . Stay alert! Watch out for your great enemy, the devil. He prowls around like a roaring lion, looking for someone to devour" (1 Pet. 5:6–8 NLT).

If you are a Christian, you believe in Satan. Why? Because Jesus did. Jesus didn't think Satan was a myth. He didn't think he was a figment of someone's imagination. He didn't think he was some cartoon character. He didn't think he was a mere projection of our minds in order to explain away the mysteries of evil. Jesus believed him to be a real, live spiritual being. He took Satan very seriously and wanted his followers to take him seriously as well. C. S. Lewis once gave a wise caution on this needed belief, writing, "There are two equal and opposite errors into which our race can fall about the devils. One is to disbelieve in their existence. The other is to believe, and to feel an excessive and unhealthy interest in them.

"They themselves," adds Lewis, "are equally pleased by both errors."[4]

Jesus's teaching on prayer seems to caution us most against the *first* of these errors—not believing in Satan and not being on guard. This is why he said to pray in a spiritually realistic way, meaning with the humility you need to be on guard against temptation and the evil one. Ask God to help you resist the temptations that will come your way that are calling you to leave the life he's called you to live. And not only that, pray that you will be protected from the schemes of the evil one, whose one and only agenda is to get you to fall into every temptation.

What Happens When We Pray?

We have been taught that there is a direct relationship between input and output. If we work a certain number of hours, we expect to reach a certain level of success. If we put our kids in the right schools, enroll them in the right programs, and do the right things as parents, we expect them to turn out right. If we invest our money strategically and wisely, we expect a fair return on our investment. Input and output. Cause and effect. The relationship between what we do and what actually takes place.

Is this what happens when we pray? Some people do not appear to think so. Author Anne Lamott writes of a friend who says for her morning prayer, "Whatever," and then for the evening, "Oh, well." The Bible encourages a slightly different attitude.[5] If there are three big takeaways, they would be these: First, God hears: "This is the assurance we have in approaching God . . . he hears us" (1 John 5:14). Second, God cares: "Give all your worries and cares to God, for he cares about you" (1 Pet. 5:7 NLT). Third, God answers: there is no such thing as unanswered prayer. And that is where I may have just lost you.

"If God answers every prayer, why is my life full of unanswered ones?

"I've prayed for a husband—still single!

"I've prayed for a job—still unemployed!

"I've prayed for healing—still sick!"

At one time or another, all of us have felt that our prayers were going unanswered. But that's what it was—a feeling. A perception. It wasn't, it *isn't* reality. In truth, God has answered—or is answering—every prayer you have ever prayed. It's just that the *way* he's answered them may not have been what you wanted or expected to hear. The way we think about prayer is like shopping on Amazon. We put various things in our cart, and then at the end, check out. Usually we get what we want the next day, no later than over the course of the next week. We can treat prayer the same way—we pray, check out with an "amen," and expect our answer package in the mail. If it doesn't come, God obviously didn't answer. The truth is that God promises to answer every prayer. *How* he chooses to answer them is another matter.

How God Answers Prayer

It's been said that when it comes to prayer, God answers in one of four ways: If the request is wrong, God says, "No"; if the timing is wrong, God says, "Slow"; if you are wrong, God says, "Grow"; but if the request is right, the timing is right, and you are right, God says, "Go!"[6] Let's walk through all four.

No

First, if the request itself is wrong, God can answer no. Ever thought about that? He's answered your prayer and said no. Some prayer requests—no matter how well-intentioned—are inappropriate, not best for you, or just plain . . . uninformed. Consider an interaction Jesus had with some of his early followers. It's recorded in Matthew 20:

> The mother of the Zebedee brothers [James and John] came with her two sons and knelt before Jesus with a request.
> "What do you want?" Jesus asked.
> She said, "Give your word that these two sons of mine will be awarded the highest places of honor in your kingdom, one at your right hand, one at your left hand."
> Jesus responded, "You have no idea what you're asking." (vv. 20–22 MSG)

> **FOUR WAYS GOD ANSWERS PRAYER**
>
> 1. NO
> 2. SLOW
> 3. GROW
> 4. GO

Good Jewish mom comes with her two boys and wants them to have the best seats in the spiritual house. Jesus not only says no but goes further: "You have no idea what you're asking!" Meaning, "If you did, you wouldn't have asked for that." The request was heard. Jesus obviously cared for her sons as they were two of his disciples! But the answer was no. Let's stay with James and John. They seemed to have a knack for wrong requests. One day Jesus and his followers were traveling to Jerusalem. One of the cities they had to go through was Samaria.

> [They] went into a Samaritan village to get things ready for him; but the people there did not welcome him. . . . When the disciples James and John saw this, they asked, "Lord, do you want us to call fire down from heaven to destroy them?" (Luke 9:52–54)

How's that for a prayer request! They didn't give us the welcome we wanted, so let's see if they love the smell of napalm in the morning. They were sincere. They felt their request made sense and was appropriate in terms of what had happened. But notice how Jesus answered: "Jesus turned on them: 'Of course not!'" (Luke 9:55 MSG). I think it makes sense that even though God hears every request and cares deeply about us, the answer can still be no.

As a father of four, I know this was true for my kids. Nobody loved them more than I did. Nobody cared about them more than I did. But sometimes they asked for things that were misguided and immature. And they didn't have a clue why! It made perfect sense to their minds to stay up all night, eat ice cream for every meal, invest significant amounts of our financial resources into the profit margin of Toys "R" Us, and establish residency at Disney World. Could it be that we are to God like our kids are to us? Is it possible that we can make requests that make perfect sense to us but in reality are shortsighted, immature, and self-serving? Or just plain injurious . . . but we don't know it? If so, then is it possible that God might just love us too much to say yes? I think that makes sense for most of us.

But some of you might be thinking, *I'm with you on how God could say no to some things, but how could it be best that somebody suffer, or even die? All I prayed for was that they would get well! How can that be so bad to ask for?* That's a fair and legitimate question. Sometimes there is nothing less than a mystery surrounding God's answers to our prayers. I've had times in my life when no matter how I looked at the request, there didn't seem to be anything wrong with it. Yet God's answer still seemed to be no. I don't have a clear, definitive answer to this mystery, and even if I did it wouldn't do much for the emotions that run with it. But let me tell you what I do know. I do know that God knows more than any of us and, ultimately, we have to settle it within ourselves as a matter of trust. That's not a cop-out, it's just a frank assessment of what the core issue really is. It all comes down to how you view the character of God. Either he's a good God or he's not. Either he can be trusted or he can't. When God seems to say no, you either believe he knows best or he doesn't.

Nothing happens to you as a Christian that does not first pass through the hands of a God wildly in love with you.

I've often shared with people a simple truth that I believe with all my heart: Nothing happens to you as a Christian that does not first pass through the hands of a God wildly in love with you. So while we may not understand it all, or know the reasons for God's answers, we can trust him, because he loves us, and loves those around us, more than we can possibly imagine. While we might not have the answer, we can trust in the one who does.

Slow

But no isn't the only way God can answer your prayers. The second way God can respond is this: if the timing is wrong, God can put on the brakes with the answer "slow." As in not now, not yet, not as fast as you're hoping for. You see, we may think we know when things should happen, but only God knows the perfect timing for our lives. So sometimes when we make a request, God says, "Not now."

This is a maddening answer to accept, because we've gotten used to microwave cooking, internet searches for instant information, the immediacy of texting . . . it's almost as if we've lost the category of "later" or "not yet," so we instantly assume "not now" is a *no*. I've had people come to me and say, "I've been praying about this thing for at least two days and God still hasn't done a thing about it!" It's so important to remember that God's timetable is always better than ours and is filled with more wisdom and insight and love for us than we could possibly imagine. He obviously has access to more information about the dynamics of our situation than we could ever begin to fathom. As God himself said through the prophet Isaiah, "My thoughts are not your thoughts, neither are your ways my ways. . . . As the heavens are higher than the earth, so are my ways higher than your ways and my thoughts than your thoughts" (Isa. 55:8–9). We need to trust in the ultimate goodness of that.

Grow

There's a third way God can answer your prayers. If the request is wrong, he can say "no." If the timing is wrong, he can say "slow." What if *you* are wrong? Then he might just say "grow." In other words, it is possible that something is wrong in our lives. That choices we've made, attitudes we have, and lifestyles we've embraced have set up a barrier between us and God. This is hard to think about, because when we think God isn't answering our prayers, or answering them the way we want him to, we automatically think that the problem lies with God. He simply must not care, or isn't fully briefed on the situation, or isn't able to perform, or just doesn't understand. What if the real problem is with the person in the mirror? What if the answer God is giving to our prayer is that we need to work on our lives?

The Bible outlines several prayer "blockers" that can stand in the way of prayer operating the way it is intended to operate between us and God. The first and most obvious prayer blocker is unconfessed sin. The prophet Isaiah stated the matter bluntly: "Your iniquities have separated you from your God; your sins have hidden his face from you, so that he will not hear" (Isa. 59:2). Unconfessed, unrepentant sin cuts off our communication with God. It shuts down the relationship. Notice the wording: It's not that God does not hear, but that he *will* not hear—he will not respond, be moved, be involved. Why? Through our unconfessed sin, we are showing complete disdain and indifference to him and our relationship with him.

Let's make sure we know what the Bible is saying here. It's not saying that you need to reach some state of perfection before God engages your prayers. It's not saying you have to be sin free. It's not about having areas where you struggle, slip up, get sloppy, or could do better. It's talking about areas where you know you are rebelling, and you don't care. You're not even authentically confronting it, much less resisting it. You've decided that you are going to do it anyway with a "to heck with it" mentality. You're going to do it whether God likes it or not, whether the Bible says it's wrong or not. According to the Bible, that's serious. Read it yourself:

> I cried out to him with my mouth. . . .
> If I had cherished sin in my heart,
>   the Lord would not have listened;
> but God has surely listened
>   and has heard my prayer. (Ps. 66:17–19)

> If anyone turns a deaf ear to my instruction,
>   even their prayers are detestable. (Prov. 28:9)

> When you spread out your hands in prayer,
>   I hide my eyes from you;
> even when you offer many prayers,
>   I am not listening. . . .

> Wash and make yourselves clean.
>   Take your evil deeds out of my sight;
>   stop doing wrong,
> Learn to do right. (Isa. 1:15–17)

Also serious is unresolved relational conflict. Here is what Jesus said:

> If you enter your place of worship and, about to make an offering, you suddenly remember a grudge a friend has against you, abandon your offering, leave immediately, go to this friend and make things right. Then and only then, come back and work things out with God. (Matt. 5:23–24 MSG)

People were coming to the temple to make a burnt offering to atone for their sins, wanting God to forgive them and to get right with God. That was good. But they were doing it as if their relationship with others didn't matter, as if a lack of love toward others, a lack of forgiveness toward others, didn't matter when it came to their relationship with God. Jesus said, "It matters. It matters so much you should seek to take care of that before you come to God about your own stuff."

A final prayer blocker worth considering has to do with selfishness. The Bible, again, puts it plainly: "When you ask, you do not receive, because you ask with wrong motives, that you may spend what you get on your pleasures" (James 4:3). If your prayers are along the lines of make me famous, make me rich, make me have a good time, make all my dreams come true, and always give me the best parking spaces, you probably aren't connecting very well with the Spirit of God. We can get creative with this and pray, "God, make me rich so I can give lots of it away." You know what the answer to that one is? If you aren't giving it away now at the level of income you have, you won't give it away then. Generosity isn't about margin; it's about spirit.

> **▶ PRAYER BLOCKERS**
>
> UNCONFESSED SIN
> UNRESOLVED
>   RELATIONAL CONFLICT
> SELFISHNESS

God Says, "Go"

What's the final way God can answer us? If the request is right, the timing is right, and you are right, God says, "Go!" He says, "Yes!" Nothing pleases God more, in this context, than to give you the desires of your heart.

I once read about a man named Bob who had a friend named Doug. Doug had a ministry in Washington, DC, among people in politics and statecraft. Bob had no connections with government at all. He was an insurance salesman. But Bob became a Christian through his friendship with Doug and began to meet with him regularly to learn about his new faith.

One day Bob came in all excited about a statement in the Bible where Jesus says to ask whatever you want in my name, and you shall receive it (John 14:14).

Bob asked Doug, "Is that really true?"

Doug said, "Well, it's not a blank check. You have to take it in the context of the teachings of the whole Scripture on prayer. But yes—it really is true. Jesus really does answer prayer."

Bob said, "Great! Then I guess I gotta start praying for something. I think I'll pray for Africa."

Doug said, "That's kind of a broad target. Why don't you narrow it down to one country?"

"All right," Bob said. "I'll pray for Kenya."

"Do you know anyone in Kenya?" Doug asked.

"Nope."

"Ever been to Kenya?"

"Nope."

Bob just wanted to pray for Kenya.

So Doug made an unusual arrangement. He challenged Bob to pray every day for six months for Kenya. If nothing extraordinary happened, Doug would pay him $500. But if something remarkable did happen, Bob would have to pay Doug $500. If Bob did not pray every day, the whole deal was off.

Not exactly your normal prayer program.

Bob took him up on it and began to pray. And for a long time, nothing happened. Then one night, he was at a dinner in Washington. The people around the table explained what they did for a living. One woman said she helped run an orphanage in Kenya, the largest of its kind in the whole nation. Bob began to ask her question after question about the orphanage and its needs and Kenya. The woman finally said, "You're obviously very interested in my country. Have you been to Kenya before?"

Bob said, "No."

"Do you know someone in Kenya?"

"No."

"Then why are you so curious?"

Then Bob said, "Well, someone is kind of paying me $500 to pray."

From that encounter, she actually asked Bob if he would like to come and visit Kenya and tour the orphanage. Bob did. When he arrived, he was appalled by the poverty and the lack of basic health care. Upon returning to Washington, he couldn't get the place out of his mind. He began to write to large pharmaceutical companies, describing the vast need he had seen. He reminded them that every year they would throw away large amounts of medical supplies that went unsold.

He asked, "Why not send them to this orphanage in Kenya?"

Some of them did. In fact, the orphanage received more than a million dollars' worth of medical supplies. The woman at the orphanage called Bob and said, "This is amazing! We've had the most phenomenal gifts because of the letters you wrote. We would like to fly you back over and have a big party. Will you come?"

So Bob flew back to Kenya.

While he was there, the president of Kenya came to the celebration, because it was the largest orphanage in the country. He met Bob and then offered to take Bob on a tour of Nairobi, the capital city. In the course of their tour, they saw a prison. Bob asked about a group of prisoners there.

The president said, "They're political prisoners."

Bob said, "That's a bad idea. You should let them out."

Bob finished the tour and flew back home. Sometime later, Bob received a phone call from the State Department of the United States government.

"Is this Bob?"

"Yes."

"Were you recently in Kenya?"

"Yes."

"Did you make any statements to the president about political prisoners?"

"Yes."

"What did you say?"

"I told him he should let them out."

The State Department official explained that his department had been working for years to get the release of those prisoners and never could. All diplomatic channels and political maneuverings had led to nothing. But now the prisoners had been released, and the State Department had learned that it was because of an insurance salesman named Bob.

They were calling to say thanks.

Several months later, the president of Kenya made a phone call to Bob. He was going to rearrange his government and select a new cabinet. He asked whether Bob would be willing to fly over and pray for him for three days while he worked on this important task. So Bob—who was not politically connected at all—boarded a plane once more and flew back to Kenya, where he prayed and asked God to give wisdom for the leader of the nation as he selected his government.[7]

Want a little adventure in *your* life?

Start praying in such a way that God will say, "Go."

REFLECTION QUESTIONS

1. Which of the seven aspects of prayer modeled by Jesus do you have the most trouble with?

2. Believers have the amazing privilege of talking directly to God in prayer. How does that make you feel?

3. How would you answer someone who asked you, "Why should I pray?"

4. Prayer can include asking God for forgiveness, thanking God, and asking God for help with problems in life. Which of these three aspects of prayer is most meaningful to you and why?

5. If you've been feeling as though God is not answering your prayers, do you have any new insights as to what his answer may really be?

CHAPTER FOUR

SPENDING TIME WITH GOD

Very early in the morning, while it was still dark,
Jesus got up, left the house and went off to a
solitary place, where he prayed.—Mark 1:35

Quick question: If you spend five minutes a day with someone, how close will you be? It's really not a trick question. The answer is simple—you will be five-minutes-a-day close. So does it matter how much time you spend each day with God? Every bit as much. Five minutes a day with God will result in being five-minutes-a-day close. No time with God at all? You can do the math.

Time is finite. I once heard it put this way: Every morning the time bank opens up an account in our name, and a little more than eighty-six thousand seconds are deposited for us to manage. Managing that time is crucial because, unlike money, there are no continuing balances, no overdrafts, and no opportunities to save for the future. We have today's deposit and that's it. If we don't use it well, then it's a total loss. We can't get it back. And to raise the stakes even higher, there is never a guarantee that another deposit will be made the next day.

Jesus and Time

When you look at the life of Jesus, you see that he was very intentional about his time with the Father. Specifically, he was intentional with how he started every single day: "Very early in the morning, while it was still dark, Jesus got up, left the house and went off to a solitary place, where he prayed" (Mark 1:35). That wasn't just a one-time observation. When you read the biographical records of his life in the Bible, you find that Jesus was very intentional about his mornings, at least when it came to his spiritual life. He went out of his way to draw from this time, to nurture it, to protect it, and to build the rhythms of his life around it.

What filled his mornings?

He began his day in prayer. He began his day orienting himself toward the eternal, the spiritual, the transcendent. He started everything with time with his Father. And it was *quality* time, involving silence and solitude. In another section of the Bible, in Luke's biography of Jesus, it says that "Jesus often slipped away to be alone so he could pray" (Luke 5:16 NCV). And then once alone, surrounded by quiet, Jesus prayed and reflected on the Scriptures.

"Jesus often slipped away to be alone so he could pray" (Luke 5:16 NCV).

We know that because we see the study of Scripture, the knowledge of Scripture, the quick and easy familiarity with Scripture, spill over into every aspect of his public life.

If you're familiar at all with the life of Jesus, you know that in the very beginning of his ministry, there was a time when he went into forty days of solitude in the wilderness, where he was tempted ferociously by Satan himself. We're given a little insight into how Jesus dealt with that temptation. He responded with the Scriptures over and over again, saying, "It is written . . . it is also written . . . it is written . . ." (Matt. 4:4, 7, 10). When he talked with people, one of his most frequent questions was, "Haven't you read [the] Scripture?" (Mark 12:10). When asked a question, he would often deal with it in the same way: "Then Jesus quoted them passage after passage from the writings of the prophets, beginning with the book of Genesis and going right on through the Scriptures, explaining what the passages meant" (Luke 24:27 TLB).

The impact of Jesus's mornings alone, praying and reflecting on the Scriptures, was profound. For example, let's go back and reread that first morning description, but continue a little bit further to see what it did for him:

> Very early in the morning, while it was still dark, Jesus got up, left the house and went off to a solitary place, where he prayed. Simon and his companions went to look for him, and when they found him, they exclaimed: "Everyone is looking for you!"
>
> Jesus replied, "Let us go somewhere else—to the nearby villages—so I can preach there also. That is why I have come." So he traveled throughout Galilee. (Mark 1:35–39)

Because of his morning time, Jesus was impacted in three very distinct ways. First, Jesus became *redirected*. He said, "I've just had my morning time with God and I now have a fresh leading as to where I should go next." He gained a clear, fresh understanding of the will of the Father for his life. It became clear what he was to do and where he was to go. Second, Jesus became *refueled*, saying, ". . . so I can preach there also." He was ready for new tasks, new challenges. Before, it was as if his spiritual tanks were running low. After his time with God the Father, he was refueled and ready to continue on with his mission. Third, Jesus became *resolved*, committed to the big picture of his priorities and life purpose. With new clarity, he could say, "This is why I have come."[1]

> **TIME WITH GOD LEAVES US . . .**
>
> REDIRECTED
> REFUELED
> RESOLVED

If you could put something into your morning routine that would redirect you in ways you need it, refuel you where you are running on empty, and give you the resolve you need to follow your life purpose, would that be worth scheduling?

Quiet Times

Every single person I know who has really developed their relationship with God and who walks with Christ in a transforming way; every person I know who leads a life of significance, impact, and influence for God; every person I know who has finished well—with their marriage, their family, with Christ at the center of it all; every person I know who, when I'm with them, gives off a sense of having the sound and smell of Jesus . . . spends time with God like this. No exceptions. They join with the psalmist, who wrote, "Every morning I lay out the pieces of my life on your altar" (Ps. 5:3 MSG).

Thomas Kelly noted that we are to live life on two levels: the level of hurried activity and then the level of the interior world. Sadly, many of us only choose to inhabit the first of these levels. The frantic race through life becomes the only plane of existence in which we operate or from which we draw. And it is a very shallow well.[2] We need the deep times, attending to the interior world of our souls.

So what does this time with God involve?

Silence and Solitude

In the movie *Nell*, Jodie Foster plays a young woman whose mother dies. After her death, Nell grows up alone in a forest, divorced from the world and its influences. She is discovered and taken out of the forest by well-meaning people who believe it is best for her to be transitioned back into the world from which she has been isolated.

As the movie develops, Nell's fate is placed into the hands of twelve jurors. After lawyers from both sides finish their closing arguments, Nell herself addresses the jury in the primitive speech she learned as a young child.

"*Yo' ha' erna lay,*" she begins.

"You have big things," another woman translates.

"*Yo known'n erna lay.*"

"You know big things."

Then, leaning toward the jury, gripping the rail that separates them, she says, "*Ma' you'nay seen inna alo'sees.*"

"But you don't look into each other's eyes."

Then the intensity of her voice rises. *"An yo'aken of a lilta-lilt."*

"And you're hungry for quietness."

Then, taking a breath as she seemingly searches for the right words, Nell continues, saying through the translator, "I've lived a small life. And I know small things. But the quiet forest is full of angels. In the daytime there comes beauty. In the nighttime, there comes happiness. Don't be afraid for Nell. Don't weep for Nell."

As Ken Gire has observed, Nell is right. We shouldn't weep for her. We should weep for ourselves. We have big things, we know big things, but we don't look into each other's eyes. And we're hungry for quietness.[3] Thomas Kelly writes of the need to go into the "recreating silences."[4] This is what we should allow our quiet times to afford us—*quiet*.

We need it.

As mentioned, I played basketball in junior high and high school, and even some into college, hoping to be a walk-on at my university. I then worked my way through the first part of my graduate school years by coaching basketball. Having been coached myself for many years and then serving as a coach, I have come to the conclusion that one of the most significant, powerful, important skills that a coach can possess is knowing when to call a time-out. There is no doubt in my mind that this ability can determine whether the game is won or lost. When you are out on the court as a player, the action is fast and furious. There isn't a lot of time to think or reflect. You just start reacting. If things start to go poorly, if the shots don't fall or the other team starts to gain the advantage, there's not a lot you can do to change things out on the court except to try to run and jump and play *harder*.

That takes energy—a lot of energy. Pretty soon, your legs feel like they're made out of lead. Then you get sloppy and start making all kinds of mistakes. It's at that point that a good coach will call a time-out. He'll stop the game and everybody will get a chance to rest, reflect, and regroup. Then, after the time-out, the team is able to go back onto the court and pick up the game where it left off. Only now, they're able to play a little better, a little smarter, and a little sharper.

It's become a different game.

In many ways, this is not only the idea behind a quiet time, but also the idea behind the sabbath rest. The Sabbath was about calling for a time-out in your life. In the fourth of the Ten Commandments, God says, "Remember the Sabbath day by keeping it holy. Six days you shall labor and do all your work, but the seventh day is a sabbath to the LORD your God. On it you shall not do any work" (Exod. 20:8–10). The word *sabbath* doesn't mean Sunday (*or* Saturday). It literally means to cease—to stop, to quit, to rest. And the word *holy* means to be something different, set apart, unique, unlike anything else. So the fourth commandment is clear: Every seven days, call a time-out. Stop the game. And then use that time for a real sabbath, a rest that will serve both you and your relationship with God.

This is why people have gathered for worship and teaching and interaction with each other at least one day a week—and usually as part of their Sabbath—from day one. This is not just about a time for a spiritual shot in the arm, but also an emotional one. It's not just about the absence of work or hurry, but the presence of that which fills you. If it's getting out on the lake, get out on the lake. If it's golfing, golf. If it's jogging, walking, playing tennis, reading, sewing, gardening, or biking . . . do it! John Ortberg described the act of sabbathing this way: "Eat foods you love to eat, listen to music that moves your soul, play a sport that stretches and challenges you, read books that refresh your spirit, wear clothes that make you happy, surround yourself with beauty—and as you do these things, give thanks to God for his wonderful goodness."[5]

This rest is important. Work and busyness and fast-paced schedules are at war against the deep issues of your life. I've always been intrigued by what God says in the forty-sixth psalm: "Be still, and know that I am God" (v. 10). How do you know God? You have to be still. Kelly is right; life is meant to be lived on two levels: the level of outward activities and the level of the interior life.[6] The temptation is to live on one level alone. This is why you have to stop long enough to let God speak to

> *"It would revolutionize the lives of most [people] if they were shut in with God in some secret place for half an hour a day."*

you, reveal himself to you, and engage you. This is also why coupling silence with solitude is so powerful. As Samuel Chadwick once observed, "It would revolutionize the lives of most [people] if they were shut in with God in some secret place for half an hour a day."[7]

There's a fascinating story from the pages of African colonial history as told by Lettie Cowman. A traveler was taking a long journey and had enlisted some of the local tribesmen to assist him in carrying his loads. The first day they moved fast and went far. But on the second day, the jungle tribesmen refused to move. They just sat and rested. The traveler, who wanted to get on with his journey, asked them why they wouldn't keep going. They told him that they had gone too fast on the first day, and that they were now *waiting for their souls to catch up with their bodies.*[8] Mrs. Cowman drew the following conclusion: "The whirling rushing life which so many of us live does for us what that first march did for those poor jungle tribesmen. The difference: *they knew* what they needed to restore life's balance; too often *we do not.*"[9]

Reflection and Meditation

But silence and solitude—for their own sake—will not nourish your soul nor enliven your intimacy with God. Your time must have content, purpose, and direction. This is the difference between Christian meditation and many forms of Eastern meditation. For the Buddhist, the goal is to empty the soul. For the Christian, the goal is to *fill* it. We must go from *detachment* to *attachment*.[10] As Dietrich Bonhoeffer once wrote, silence is "nothing else but waiting for God's Word and coming from God's Word with a blessing."[11]

This involves three primary activities: reading the Word of God, reflecting on the Word of God, and then responding to the Word of God. *Reading* simply involves using your eyes to take in what is on the surface. *Reflecting* on the Word of God engages your mind to see what is beneath the surface. *Responding* to the Word is giving what we have seen a place to live within our heart.[12] As Ken Gire has noted, reading the Word without taking time to reflect on it would be like sitting at a table where a sumptuous meal has been prepared and eyeing all the food but never eating. And reflecting on the Word without prayerfully responding to it would be like chewing the food but never swallowing.[13] The Word of God comes in the "recreating silences," but we must determine whether we will let it "recreate" us.

As I've written in other places, this is actually a very ancient practice known as *lectio divina* that was once common among all Christians.[14] The idea was to read the Bible slowly, contemplatively, in order to enable the Scriptures to penetrate and afford a union with God. Our thoughts with his; our heart with his. As Benedict suggested in the prologue to his Rule, the goal is to hear "with the ear of your heart,"[15] to attune ourselves to the "gentle whisper" of the word of the Lord (1 Kings 19:12). Much like dry, hardened soil is unable to absorb a torrential downpour, we need to let the Word of God gently rain on our parched soul so that we are able to soak in every drop. This means less volume, but more life change. And the goal is not speed-reading but listening. It is being like Mary, who "pondered . . . in her heart" all that she had seen and heard of Christ (Luke 2:19). The process is simple but takes enormous intent: We listen deeply by reading from the Scriptures; we meditate on what we have read in such a way that it interacts with the deepest parts of who we are; we pray through what we are hearing so that it is *applied* to the deepest parts of who we are; and finally, through contemplation we "rest in the presence of the One who has used His word as a means of inviting us to accept His transforming embrace."[16]

If we are willing to follow this process, the impact on our life should not be underestimated. The first psalm notes that the person who leads a blessed life not only delights in the law of the Lord but meditates on it day and night in order that it might guide his steps and serve as his counsel. Result? "That person is like a tree planted by streams of water, which yields its fruit in season and whose leaf does not wither—whatever they do prospers" (v. 3).

Listening

But mere silence and solitude, reflection and meditation, is not all that's involved in a quiet time. Our time with God must be coupled with active and intent *listening*. As we quiet ourselves and reflect on God's Word to us through the Scriptures, we will experience God speaking to our lives. This is more than responding to the Word in terms of obedience. The quieting of your life and heart, coupled with reflection and meditation on the Word of God, will result in God *impressing* himself upon you, giving guidance, direction, prompting, and insight. As the Bible reminds us, "Our God comes and will not be silent" (Ps. 50:3). Few verses are as poignant as those in the first chapter of Proverbs, where God says, "If only you had listened . . . I would have told you what's in my heart; I would have told you what I am thinking. I called, but you refused to listen" (vv. 23–24 NCV).

A way of capturing this "listening" often involves journaling, keeping a written record of thoughts and prayers to God that flow from your quiet times. I confess that I have had a difficult relationship with journaling over the years, feeling awkward by its recorded, public-like nature. I was far too self-conscious to pour out my private thoughts and feelings on paper, for fear that the journals would be found and read. I also felt that if I journaled, I would be tempted to write as if one day the journals would be found, thereby adopting a false and unrealistic tone to ensure my reputation among those who might read them. Yet I never could quite get away from the *idea* of journaling, however much I may have chafed at the thought of the practice of the discipline. Many Christians have found journaling to be a valid practice, and many men and women I respected were greatly served by it.

> "If only you had listened . . . I would have told you what's in my heart; I would have told you what I am thinking. I called, but you refused to listen" (Prov. 1:23–24 NCV).

So I began keeping a journal, but on my own terms. For many Christians, journaling is the pouring out of every thought and every prayer, creating a running spiritual diary. For me, it is simply a place to capture what I sense God is trying to tell me, to do with me, to reveal to me about myself and himself. When such spiritual insights come, they are precious. In the past, I had scribbled these insights down on random pieces of paper, kept them tucked away in a file on my desk or in a drawer, but they were soon lost or forgotten. I have come to realize that I simply cannot afford this. They will only serve my spiritual growth if they are grouped together, available for review, reflection, remembrance, and, most importantly, continued application. So yes, I journal. And you might want to as well.

Prayer

The final component to time with God is prayer, which is communication, conversation, and communion with the living God. We've already explored this in a previous chapter, but in terms of your quiet time, prayer can be guided by many things, not the least of which is your response to the Word from God received through your time *with* the Word, resulting in confession or gratitude, praise or request. Yet prayer must not simply be responsive—it must also be intentional and proactive.

I've followed a little guideline for many, many years. It may not work for you—you may actually want something less structured, just a free flow of thoughts and feelings and impressions. But for me, I enjoy walking through a certain rhythm when I pray, and this has given me that construct. Whenever I pray I actually mentally walk through these four things, not unlike bringing notes into an important meeting so you won't forget anything. It's built off of the acrostic A-C-T-S, and it helps me remember how to pray.

A is for adoration.
C is for confession.
T is for thanksgiving.
S is for supply.

Start off with **A**—adoration. Spend some time expressing your feelings for God. Tell him what's in your heart toward him. I'm very comfortable as a Christ follower telling God I love him. You may not be there yet. Yes, you feel it, but expressing it may be awkward. That's okay—just give God the honor due him.

Next is the **C**. Confess your sins, along the lines discussed in the earlier chapter. Specifically. Get them out there and before him with absolute honesty. Not in a neurotic, self-flagellating, paranoid, laundry-list way, but in an authentic way that expresses key things you know you want to confess, things that stand out in your spirit, as well as a blanket statement at the end to ask him to forgive you for all your sins.

So that's the **A** and the **C**. Now for the **T**. Spend some time thanking God for all he's done in your life. The Bible says that every good and perfect gift comes from him (James 1:17). Every good and perfect thing in your life is a God thing. So thank him for these things. That should come easy.

Thank him for being alive.

Thank him for those you love and who love you.

Thank him for a roof over your head.

Finally, tell him what's on your mind, asking for his help. This is the **S**—supply. Every one of us has needs—areas where God's supply would be like the cavalry arriving. Ask for his help for the challenges of the day, the needs of the day, the anxieties and worries and fears of the day. The needs of those in your orbit you know have their own sets of challenges and worries. He's told us to ask, so ask.

Building a Quiet Time into Your Life

How do you build this into your life? Enormous help can be found through a man named Daniel, who led an extraordinary life recorded for us in the Bible. During his time, Daniel was one of the top three men in the government of the world's largest empire, personally responsible for forty districts of the kingdom, constituting one-third of the entire land. To put ourselves in his shoes, I have heard it described as being personally responsible for governing all of the states in America east of the Mississippi River. Daniel was so good at his job, so committed and invested, that the king eventually placed him in charge of the *entire* kingdom. Daniel was a very busy man, and he managed his responsibilities with the highest level of effectiveness. Yet notice this passing observation about his schedule: "Daniel . . . went home and knelt down as usual in his upstairs room, with its windows opened toward

Jerusalem. He prayed three times a day, just as he had always done, giving thanks to his God" (Dan. 6:10 NLT).

Daniel was a man who had built a regular time with God into his life. He never let it get sidelined, marginalized, or put on the shelf. So how did he do it? First, Daniel included his quiet time in his schedule. It wasn't something he left to chance. He prioritized it. In fact, the Bible tells us that he had three set times a day for it, with a planned place to go each time. The Bible also notes that not only did he have a specific time and place for his quiet time, but Daniel made an ongoing investment in this time. Did you notice the language? The Bible says that Daniel "went home and knelt down *as usual . . . just as he had always done*" (emphasis mine). Spending time with God was a pattern for Daniel's life—not in a legalistic way, but in a disciplined, committed way.

So how can we follow Daniel's pattern?

Set a Time

First, set a time. It really is something you should schedule. For me, it's early in the mornings. I'm up every day at 4:30. It's when I'm at my best. But since this is time for you and God, I would suggest that the best time for you is when *you* are at your best. Meaning when you are most alert, most energetic, most alive, and most engaged. For most people, that's at the start of the day—not the end, when you're tired, worn out, and can barely keep your eyes open. And as Jesus modeled, there's something about starting your day *with* God that shapes your day *for* God. But whether or not morning is the best time for you, the important thing is to set a time.

Find a Place

Second, find a specific place. You may think that this is being way too detailed, but you really do need to have a place that becomes your "just you and God" space that you go to. It may be in your office with the door closed. It may be at the kitchen table or in a rocker on your porch. For me, it's in a darkened room, in a chair, before a window. The key is to find a place where you can be alone and uninterrupted.

Have a Plan

Third, have a plan for your time. Know what it is you're going to do. This is not about being legalistic with your quiet time—it's all about maximizing this time to its fullest potential. Here's what I would suggest, particularly if you're just starting out. Start off with just seven minutes.[17] Five minutes is probably too short, and ten minutes may be too long at first, so begin with seven. Also, the length ensures it will happen, because who can't find seven minutes a day to give to God?

I know what you're thinking. Nothing that short can really matter, can it? Actually, yes it can. Think about football. All through training camp, teams work on the two-minute drill, a carefully crafted set of plays to be used when the game is close and the two-minute warning has been sounded. At that moment, everything becomes focused on clock management, maximizing the number of plays and employing a hurry-up offense in order to score and win the game. Managing players, substitutions, time-outs, employing clock-stopping plays such as a pass to the sidelines so that they can get out of bounds—those two minutes can hold a lot. Why do they work on it so hard, more than almost any other drill? Because those two minutes matter in a disproportionate way. They can be where the game is won or lost. So don't underestimate seven minutes with God. It can be a seven-minute drill that can revolutionize your life.

> **7 MINUTES WITH GOD**
>
> 30 SECONDS: PREPARING YOUR HEART
> 4 MINUTES: READING THE BIBLE
> 2 ½ MINUTES: PRAYING

The First Thirty Seconds: Preparing Your Heart

Start off with thirty seconds, spending it by preparing your heart and turning inward. This is necessary because we all tend to live on the surface of life with all of the activity and noise and distractions. So put the phone away. Then use the time to maybe thank God for a good night's sleep or thank him for a new day to live. Something that brings your thinking and spirit below the surface of things. In that thirty seconds, ask him to open up your heart so that you can be responsive to what he might say to you through prayer or what you read. Ask him to be with you, to meet with you, to speak to you, and to teach you.

Just thirty seconds.

Say, "God, I'm here. Be with me."

The Next Four Minutes: Reading the Bible

Then, in the next four minutes, take out your Bible and read it. I wouldn't worry about studying it at this point, important as that is. In the beginning, for your quiet time, just read it devotionally. There are "through the Bible in a year" devotional guides that lead you to read a section from the Old Testament, a section from the New Testament, and a portion of a psalm or a proverb or two each day. You may just want to start reading through John as we talked about in the earlier chapter on the Bible. It doesn't really matter as long as you take these four minutes and do nothing but read Scripture, slowly, thoughtfully, through the lens of your heart as if this really is God's Word to you . . . because it is.

The Final Two and a Half Minutes: Praying

After you've spent four minutes reading the Bible, allowing God to talk to you, then spend two and a half minutes praying, allowing you to talk to God. Even though it's just two and a half minutes, it may be longer than you have ever prayed in your life. And if you follow the A-C-T-S model I introduced earlier, you'll find that the time flies. Just go through adoration, confession, thanksgiving, and supply. I do this every morning, and it keeps me focused as I pray.

Now, as for the seven minutes a day, I would try for at least three days a week, then let that grow to five or more. As you consistently spend the seven minutes, you'll find that they naturally become ten, and then twelve, and then fifteen. Before you know it you're effortlessly spending twenty to thirty minutes with God, time you will feast off of for the rest of the day. And God will meet you—every time. Because while this time is needed for you and your spiritual life, it's precious to him. He loves you—you're his son; you're his daughter. And you're prioritizing spending time with him.

Many years ago, my oldest daughter, Rebecca, went through a time when she got up very early in the morning. Even before me. When she did, she would get out of her bed, come into Susan's and my bedroom, walk over to my side of the bed, tap me on the shoulder, and whisper, "Daddy, come be with me. Come be with me, Daddy." Now how do you think I felt when this precious four-year-old, in her little nightgown and holding her favorite stuffed animal, stood by my bed and said she wanted to be with her daddy? I melted. And I got the heck out of that bed. Then we'd be together—just the two of us. How could I say no? How can you turn down someone you love who just wants time with you? And I can't even begin to tell you what those times did for our relationship.

I think that every morning you get up and say, "Abba, come be with me," the heart of God melts. And you can count on him being right there . . . and the two of you getting very, very close.

REFLECTION QUESTIONS

1. Why is it important for believers to spend time with God each day?

2. What time of day do you find it easiest to concentrate on God?

3. What places do you find most conducive for spending time with God (e.g., a back porch)?

4. We often tend to think about meditation being associated with Eastern religious practices. How do you think the idea of Christian meditation could change your time with God?

5. It seems incredible that God really wants us to tell him exactly what is weighing on our minds. What does that tell you about God?

CHAPTER FIVE

EXPERIENCING LIFE IN COMMUNITY

Let him who is not in community beware of being alone.—Dietrich Bonhoeffer[1]

If you want to go fast, go alone. If you want to go far, go together.—African proverb

The first time I traveled to the famed American port city of Boston, I built time into my schedule to tour its well-known sites. I followed the famous Red Line through the heart of the city's historical district, made my way to the waterfront, walked the naval yard where my father had been stationed during the Korean War, and spent some time at the Commons. But I confess that what I *really* wanted to find was a bar! The Bull & Finch Pub to be exact. You may know it by another name—Cheers.

The Bull & Finch Pub was the inspiration for the hit TV series *Cheers*, which remains one of my favorite series ever. While still popular on Netflix, younger readers will be more familiar with its lead actor, Ted Danson, as the demon-turned-good architect of *The Good Place*. But during its run in the eighties and into the nineties, *Cheers* earned 28 Primetime Emmy Awards from a (then) record of 117 nominations.[2]

So while I was in Boston, I wanted to see the real thing. And I did. I went in, ate lunch, and had a great time. As I was walking out, I began to think about all of the things that made me like that series—the memorable characters, the funny stories, the great one-liners. But it clicked with me that what I liked most was something deeper. In truth, I was drawn to the sense of *community*. At Cheers, everybody seemed to *care* about each other, *support* each other, and *accept* each other's weaknesses. It was the kind of place you'd like to be able to just go to and hang out. Even the theme song, which was almost as popular as the show itself, made you feel this way: "You want to be where everybody knows your name."[3]

There's something about community—the relationships, the sense of belonging, the support and encouragement, the sympathy and understanding—that deepens our lives and anchors our souls. But the community pictured in shows like *Cheers* or *Friends*, or more recently in *This Is Us* or *Stranger Things*, pales in comparison to the truest, best, clearest picture of community that has ever been presented—the *new* community, called together by Christ for Christ, better known as the church. And no better snapshot of its life can be found than in the second chapter of Acts:

> They devoted themselves to the apostles' teaching and to fellowship, to the breaking of bread and to prayer. Everyone was filled with awe at the many wonders and miraculous signs performed by the apostles. All the believers were together and had everything in common. They sold property and possessions to give to anyone who had need. Every day they continued to meet together in the temple courts. They broke bread in their homes and ate together with glad and sincere hearts, praising God and enjoying the favor of all the people. And the Lord added to their number daily those who were being saved. (vv. 42–47)

In this portrait, we find that the new community that Christ came to establish is a place where there is love, intimacy, service, and honor. A place, as it has often been said, where you can love and be loved, know and be known, serve and be served, celebrate and be celebrated. Those are four things that are marks of this new community and that are *indispensable* to a life in Christ.[4]

Love and Be Loved

The first mark of the new community is that it is a place where you can love and be loved. In writing the history of the early church, Luke observed, "They devoted themselves to the . . . fellowship" (Acts 2:42). The word he used for "fellowship" was the Greek word *koinonia*, which has to do with companionship, sharing, and being connected with another person in intimacy. It is the expression of enthusiastic love. People were taking the "high road" with each other, never assuming the worst or giving in to suspicion. True *koinonia* is when people are completely upheld, completely accepted, and completely supported. "To love a person," said the great Russian novelist Dostoevsky, "means to see him as God intended him to be."[5]

Know and Be Known

Not only did Luke say that they were devoted to the fellowship, he also noted that "all the believers were together and had everything in common" (Acts 2:44). They were sharing, talking, revealing—they were not holding anything back. The truth is that we all have weaknesses. A true community allows people to stand up and say, "My name is John, and I'm struggling with porn; my name is Betty, and I have breast cancer; my name is Steve, and my marriage is falling apart; my name is Carol, and I

> **THE MARKS OF THE NEW COMMUNITY**
>
> LOVE AND BE LOVED
> KNOW AND BE KNOWN
> SERVE AND BE SERVED
> CELEBRATE AND BE CELEBRATED

just lost my job; my name is Alice, and I'm lonely." Community is not simply being able to reveal who we are, but for that revelation to be in *safe hands*. Knowledge of one another in the new community is not the basis for wounding, but for healing through the giving and receiving of grace, love, and support.

Serve and Be Served

The third mark of the new community is that it is a place where you can serve and be served. When Luke described the early church, he noted, "They sold property and possessions to give to anyone who had need" (Acts 2:45). There was a spirit of giving to each other at points of need in the community. Do you have a group of people in your life who really know you, really care about you, really love you, and are committed to your spiritual growth and development?

A young woman in our church experienced the horror of being diagnosed with breast cancer. After the cancer was discovered, it was considered advanced enough to require a radical mastectomy. She was quickly surrounded by prayer and support, phone calls and texts, Facebook postings and meals, and all the counsel and advice her network of medical friends and family could provide. As I drove to the hospital for a room visit, I passed by multiple members of the church in the parking lot on my way in who had stopped by as well. When the ordeal was over she expressed to me how she couldn't have imagined going through it without a church family—how isolating it would've felt without the support of her community of faith.

A young couple in our church became involved in one of our small groups. The husband had just moved to Charlotte to start his own landscape maintenance company, so the company was in a fragile start-up phase. In working with a lawn mower one day, he had an accident. His hand got caught in the mower, and he lost part of a finger. That was bad enough in itself, but it also meant that he faced the possibility of losing a lot more. He couldn't use his hand for several weeks, so he couldn't work. Because the business had just started, he couldn't afford to hire extra help. And if the work didn't get done, he'd lose contracts and his whole business could go under. That's when his small group stepped in. They pitched in and took turns doing his work for him. Individuals in his group used vacation days from their jobs so they could work his contracts. They stepped in and became a work crew. Because they were willing to serve one of their own in need, he is in business to this day.

Celebrate and Be Celebrated

A final mark of the new community is that it is where you can celebrate and be celebrated. Notice how Luke ended his summary: "They broke bread in their homes and ate together with glad and sincere hearts, praising God and enjoying the favor of all the people. And the Lord added to their number daily those who were being saved" (Acts 2:46–47). They were being together and enjoying it. They were in each other's homes, sharing meals, laughing and talking, celebrating life with each other and with God. It was so good that other people who weren't even Christians wanted to *be* Christians because of the community!

Disappointment with the Church

Sounds good, doesn't it? But many of you are saying, "That's not the church I know about." I have a feeling that a lot of you are thinking, *Community, yes. Church, no*. I get it and have written extensively about it in other books.[6]

While the church can, at times, be a dysfunctional expression of the community it was intended to be, it continues to have a clear and compelling vision that shapes it toward health and wholeness in a way unlike any other gathering. Jesus came to establish a *new* community of people. He said, "I will build *my* church" (Matt. 16:18, emphasis mine). Jesus wanted the church to be full of people who are allowed and encouraged to be *real* with each other, opening themselves up for care and love and support. The new community that Jesus initiated was to be built on healthy, deep, loving relationships forged on the anvil of conflict resolution. The new community that Jesus came to establish was to be marked by a spirit of *acceptance*, one that looks at people— imperfections and all—and receives them for who they are and how God made them. Most people find that when they explore the vision for church that Jesus and the Bible describe, it isn't church *itself* they are turned off to, but the way people have been *doing* church. And while many churches fall short of this vision, countless others are *decisively* marked by the biblical portrait of the church as the new community. When you find a church like that and invest in it, you will discover the community that you long for and desperately need.

The lie is that we can do life on our own. The truth is that we can't. If we don't bond with people, we become emotionally and spiritually dysfunctional. *Seriously* dysfunctional. The results of a study conducted in 1945 are still fascinating. The study looked at infants in institutions. The physical needs of all the babies were met. They were fed when they were hungry, and their diapers were changed when they were wet. However, because of the shortage of caretakers, only some of the babies were regularly held and talked to. The ones who were *not* held showed drastically higher rates of illness—and even death. Additionally, their psychological development was either slowed or stopped. All because of one thing: a lack of emotional, *relational* bonding.[7]

This is true spiritually, as well.

John Stott tells of a Scottish minister who visited a church member who had drifted away from the community of the church. Upon entering the home, the minister sat down with the man in his den before the fireplace. Neither said a word. Finally, the minister leaned forward, picked up the fireplace tongs, and took a burning coal from the fire. He laid the coal off to the side and, in just a few moments, what was once a bright, burning coal turned to cold, gray ash and eventually went out altogether. Then the minister picked it back up and put it with the other coals. Within a few seconds, it was on fire again. Then the minister got up and left the man. Neither said a word through the entire visit, but the point was made. The next weekend, the man returned to his family of faith.[8]

Signing On

So how do you experience the rewards of the new community? By joining one! You cannot develop yourself spiritually to the degree God intends apart from others. This is why finding a community—and committing to it—is one of the most important spiritual steps you can take. Apart from life in community with other believers, you can't practice the "one anothers" that lie at the heart of not only community, but spiritual growth. Here's a sampling of those directives:

Be devoted to one another. (Rom. 12:10)

Live in harmony with one another. (Rom. 12:16)

Be patient, bearing with one another in love. (Eph. 4:2)

Spur one another on toward love and good deeds. (Heb. 10:24)

Accept one another. (Rom. 15:7)

Stop passing judgment on one another. (Rom. 14:13)

Be kind and compassionate to one another. (Eph. 4:32)

Therefore encourage one another. (1 Thess. 5:11)

Forgive one another if any of you has a grievance against someone. (Col. 3:13)

Offer hospitality to one another. (1 Pet. 4:9)

And then, over and over again in Scripture you find this phrase, first uttered by Jesus himself:

Love one another. (John 13:34)

Which of these can be experienced, much less pursued, outside of community? Not a single one.

This is why joining a church—yes, becoming a member—is an important step to take. The Bible teaches that "we, though many, form one body, and each member belongs to all the others" (Rom. 12:5). Even further, the Bible says that, as a Christian, "you are members of God's very own family . . . and you belong in God's household with every other Christian" (Eph. 2:19 TLB). That last verse holds three key truths: first, that the church is a family; second, that God expects Christians to be members of a church family; and third, that a Christian without a church family is a contradiction![9] Not only does becoming a member of a local church community express obedience to the Bible, but it also moves us into a position of committed participation. It presents an opportunity to "step out of the stands" and publicly assert our commitment to Christ and to a specific local faith community. In this sense, membership can be one of the most significant and defining moments in your spiritual life. Yet while membership in a church brings you into the

> **THREE KEY TRUTHS**
>
> 1. THE CHURCH IS A FAMILY.
> 2. GOD EXPECTS CHRISTIANS TO BE MEMBERS OF A CHURCH FAMILY.
> 3. A CHRISTIAN WITHOUT A CHURCH FAMILY IS A CONTRADICTION.

new community, it is only the *entrance*. The *power* of relational life must still be seized.

The Power of Relationships

Think about your answer to this question: If two horses can pull nine thousand pounds, how many pounds can four horses pull? If you thought nine thousand pounds, you were wrong. If you thought eighteen thousand pounds, you were wrong. The answer is that while two horses can pull nine thousand pounds, four horses can pull more than *thirty thousand* pounds. Now if that doesn't make sense, it's because you haven't been introduced to the concept of synergy.

Synergy is the energy or force that is generated through the working together of various parts or processes. In his classic economics text *The Wealth of Nations*, Adam Smith wrote that ten people working individually can produce twenty pins a day, but ten people working *together* can produce *forty-eight thousand* pins a day. Synergy is bigger than just tasks, production, or the weight you can pull. It has to do with every aspect of life. Married couples will talk about the benefits of a counselor. Athletes will talk about the importance of a trainer or a coach. Businesspeople will talk about the power of a team. This concept is true for your spiritual life as well. When you start developing strategic, spiritual relationships in your life, the impact is phenomenal, beginning with the *challenge* these relationships bring to your life.

Challenge

Nothing pushes me, motivates me, or influences me more than being around someone who is operating at a higher level than I am—someone who is stronger than I am, more developed than I am, has accomplished more than I have, or has a depth of character exceeding my own. When I'm around that kind of person, it makes me want to commit myself more deeply, pay attention to areas I've ignored, and deepen my walk with God. It makes me want to elevate my game to a new level.

Soon after my appointment to the presidency of Gordon-Conwell Theological Seminary, I received a phone call inviting me and my wife, Susan, to a visit with Billy and Ruth Graham at their home in the Blue Ridge Mountains of Montreat, North Carolina. Billy had been instrumental in the establishment of the school, along with Harold Ockenga and J. Howard Pew, and I was to be only the fourth president in the school's already storied history. As Susan and I were escorted to their rustic mountain retreat, past the old moonshiner's cabin Ruth chose to keep intact from earlier owners, we discovered we had more in store than an afternoon with a man and woman who had been used by God to influence the wider evangelical world more than any other figures in the twentieth century.

I was nervous enough to have missed a firm grip in our initial handshake. Billy laughed and said that was how Eisenhower shook hands every time. Billy began to reminisce and tell stories. I asked him for the founding vision of the seminary and the many other institutions that he helped shape: *Christianity Today* magazine, Fuller Theological Seminary, Wheaton College, the National Association of Evangelicals, the Lausanne Movement, and more. The vision for each was the same. As he began his world travels, Billy found that Christians around the world did not know one another, and he felt God impress upon his heart to bring them together. That, he said, was one of the principal reasons he wanted to see such institutions founded. There needed to be a place where evangelicals could get to know one another, be brought together, build relationships, and form the alliances needed to impact the world for Christ. Fragmented, there would never be the synergy and strength needed to bring the gospel to bear on the world.

There is more that could be said of that day.

Billy, using his walker, showed me around the house that Ruth had almost single-handedly constructed from odds and ends found rummaging around yard sales and auctions. Our time ended with him taking me into his study where he had written his sermons for the crusades that reached millions. Littered throughout were pictures of family, as well as of men who had influenced his life—all now gone to be with the God they had given their lives to serve.

I was touched, as so many before me, by his humility and genuine grace. But even more by his passionate love for Ruth, who sadly passed away just a few short months after our visit.

Following an hour or so of conversation, he walked us back to the bedroom where Ruth was confined to bed. She had gamely prepared to receive us and had been moved to a nearby chair next to a low-lying bookshelf where notebooks containing books of the Bible had been prepared for her with oversized type so that she could read them despite her failing eyesight. They talked of their nightly devotions with one another, how they prayed for their children, and how those who said there was no romance at their age were wrong.

"We have romance through our eyes," Billy explained.

He was right. They did.

He seemed far more honored to entertain us in his home than we were to be entertained. He insisted on walking us to the door and stood waving at our car until we were out of sight down the steep mountain road.

A single afternoon. Years later, as I attended his funeral with presidents and dignitaries and celebrities at hand, I remembered the time I spent with him. It may be what affected me most about his life.

This is the idea—again—behind the Bible's admonition: "As iron sharpens iron, so one person sharpens another" (Prov. 27:17). Iron against iron—the clang, the noise, the sparks, and the contact. You can feel the idea of challenge coming through. And that's what keeps us sharp.

Encouragement

A second payoff from strategic, spiritual relationships has to do with *encouragement*. We read this earlier, but the words from Scripture bear repeating: "Let us consider how we may spur one another on toward love and good deeds, not giving up meeting together, as some are in the habit of doing, but encouraging one another" (Heb. 10:24–25). We all need people who come alongside us and help us keep going.

Some time ago I was going through a difficult time. I was tired and emotionally depleted. I don't often talk about such things with others—my tendency is to hold it in and soldier through. But once, during one of my messages, I made a slight reference to my emotional state at the beginning of the talk—just something minor like, "Boy, I needed that time of worship today because, like many of you, I've had a long week, and that was just a shot in the arm." The next day, a friend of mine in the church came by my office with a large cup stuffed with candy and tied up in ribbons, with a card attached to it. Inside that card was written, "Jim: From what you said at church, you are having a rough week. Hope this cheers you up. So many people, including myself, would not be walking with Christ if it weren't for you and your dedication to the mission. Thanks for serving the Lord with your gift of leadership."

I needed that. We all do.

Accountability

Another dynamic that relationships bring is *accountability*. Socrates once contended that the unexamined life was not worth living. It could be said that the unexamined *spiritual* life is not *able* to be lived. When it comes to our spirituality, only so much is able to be self-inspected. Chuck Colson wrote of the power that accountable relationships brought to his life, particularly his regular gatherings with a small group of men for the purpose of sharing and dialogue—conversation that included asking each other the following seven questions:[10]

1. Have you been with a woman anywhere this past week that might be seen as compromising?
2. Have any of your financial dealings lacked integrity?
3. Have you exposed yourself to any sexually explicit material?
4. Have you spent adequate time in Bible study and prayer?
5. Have you given priority time to your family?
6. Have you fulfilled the mandates of your calling?
7. Have you just lied to me?

Accountability should never become a euphemism for control or for creating a legalistic, oppressive existence that causes you to live in fear and bondage. Being accountable is simply living a life that allows others to see the inside so that they can bring objective counsel and helpful challenge.

Support

A final contribution that relationships often bring has to do with support. The Bible says, "Two are better than one, because they have a good return for their labor: If either of them falls down, one can help the other up. But pity anyone who falls and has no one to help them up" (Eccles. 4:9–10). Challenge is needed. Encouragement is needed. But so is *support*, somebody who can provide help. Someone who can put their arm around you and help you make it through those times you cannot stand on your own.

Henry Cloud tells of a friend of his who called him and said, "Sorry to call so late. . . . I'm broke. . . . Somebody has embezzled everything I have, and I'm really in trouble. I have been investing with a money manager for about a year, and it looks like he has taken all my liquid cash. . . . Can you meet me for lunch next Thursday at the club?"

What was particularly heartbreaking was that only a few months earlier, this man's wife had left him and had taken their children with her. So now he was stripped of everything—his wife, his children, and his money.

The day for the lunch came, and Henry found out that his friend had invited others as well, assembling a small group of his closest friends. Once gathered around the table, he said, "Guys, I'm busted. It looks like I have lost everything. It is really bleak. But here's what I need from you. If each of you will sign up for a day a week to have lunch with me, if I know that I will see one of you every day, I can make my comeback. If I know that I have your support, then I can do it."

They all answered that he could count on them, and in about eighteen months he had done it. He was back on his feet financially and spiritually. But it took some people who were willing to just *live* with him—to go through it with him.[11]

Such stories are testimony to Dietrich Bonhoeffer's declaration that simply the "physical presence of other Christians is a source of incomparable joy and strength to the believer."[12] Or as Anne Lamott has written, "No matter how bad I am feeling, how lost or lonely or frightened, when I see faces of the people at my church, and hear their tawny voices, I can always find my way home."[13]

Adding Relationships to Your Life

So how do you develop strategic spiritual relationships within the new community? On purpose. This means you begin by taking a relational inventory.

Relational Inventory

It has been said that what you will be like in five years is based on two things: the books you read and the people you spend time with. It is difficult to underestimate the impact of the people who surround you.

I once heard one of my college professors make a passing reference to a marketing study of teenagers. Apparently several high school students were asked to give their opinions regarding a particular style of jeans. Overwhelmingly, the students thought that they were the ugliest jeans they had ever seen! The researchers waited a few months and then went back to the same high school. They took key opinion leaders—the captain of the basketball team, the head cheerleader, the first-string quarterback, the homecoming queen, and the student body president—gave each one a pair of the jeans, and asked them to wear them regularly to school for a month without telling anyone why they were choosing to wear the new style. By the end of the month, stores were besieged by students wanting to know where they could find the new fashion.

The influence of others doesn't diminish as we grow older. Baseball fans are familiar with the name of Casey Stengel, famed former manager of the New York Yankees. When Billy Martin took over as manager, Stengel had some interesting advice for him. He said, "Billy, on any team there will be fifteen guys who will run through a wall for you, five who will hate you, and five who are undecided." Stengel then said, "When you make out your rooming list, always room your losers together. Never room a good guy with a loser. *It won't spread if you keep them isolated.*"[14]

If you are surrounded by spiritually positive and healthy people, you will find your *own* spiritual life and development boosted. The opposite is equally true—there are those who can actually *weaken* you spiritually, lowering your commitment and resolve. This is the importance of maintaining a relational inventory in your life at all times. This is not meant to exclude people who need our influence. As John Maxwell has wisely pointed out, there is a difference between helping those with perpetual attitude problems and enlisting them as our close friends. The closer our relationships, the more influential their attitudes and philosophies become to us.[15]

Consider the life of Jesus. He cared about everyone, but there were certain people whom he was drawn to relationally. For example, Jesus pulled Peter, James, and John off to the side to be with him at spiritually important times, such as the raising of a little girl from the dead, as well as the transfiguration where Moses and Elijah came and spoke with Jesus. It was also Peter, James, and John whom Jesus called to be with him at his most difficult times, such as in the Garden of Gethsemane the night before his crucifixion. You could also make a case that Mary, Martha, and Lazarus were important to Jesus in terms of strategic relationships. An interesting statement in the Gospel of John says, "Jesus loved Martha and her sister [Mary] and Lazarus" (11:5). In fact, Jesus seemed to purposefully orient his travel plans in order to stay at their house. Jesus modeled life as it was meant to be lived, and he understood that some people *feed* you, and some people feed *off* of you. You need a balance of both for spiritual health.

So here's the critical question: *Are those around you, in your innermost circle, bringing you closer to Jesus or taking you further away?* In taking your own relational inventory, begin with the three basic types of people in your life—those who drain you, those who are neutral, and those who put gas in your spiritual tanks. Or as one friend of mine put it, first there are **VIPs**—Very Important People. These people ignite your passion and faith for living more like Jesus. They make a very significant contribution to who you are and what you are doing. They mentor you, challenge you, invest in you, model things for you. You walk away from time spent with them energized, en-

▶ **TAKE A RELATIONAL INVENTORY**

VIP—VERY IMPORTANT PEOPLE

VNP—VERY NEUTRAL PEOPLE

VDP—VERY DRAINING PEOPLE

visioned, ready to try new things and reach new heights. They spur you on.

Next are **VNPs**—Very Neutral People. They may enjoy your spiritual passion, but they don't do much to stimulate yours. Neutral people can be fun to have around, they can boost your ego, but they don't add much to the spiritual mix. You have to be careful about VNPs—they can seem innocent, innocuous, harmless. But over time, a VNP may allow you to drift toward the course of least resistance, and their own passivity, their own lack of passion, will lead you to lower your own expectations, so that you care less, aspire to less, and achieve less.

And then there are **VDPs**—Very Draining People. They are the ones who sap your passion. They drain away your enthusiasm, your commitment, your heart for serving Christ.[16] At some point, take a relational inventory. Take out a piece of paper and make three columns—one for VIPs, one for VNPs, and one for VDPs. Then scroll through your relational world, particularly your inner circle, and put the names of those closest to you into the appropriate category. Be ruthlessly honest about this, and don't worry about the estimation of others while doing it. One person's VDP may be somebody else's VIP. In the Bible we find that the apostle Paul (at least initially) had a hard time with Mark, while Barnabas gladly invested time and energy into Mark's life. The point is to take an inventory of who those people are for *you*—the feelings that spending time with them bring out in you.

If you don't have many VIPs, but a lot of VNPs or VDPs, you have some relational work to do.

Intentionally Find and Develop Mentors

The second step in adding strategic, spiritual relationships is to use this inventory to intentionally find and develop your relationships with people who you know positively impact your spiritual life. Spend time with them. Knit your hearts and lives together. Let them challenge, encourage, and support you, as you do the same for them. Then look for those who can become even more strategic—those who might be able to become something of a mentor.

Mentoring is how most people used to be trained and developed for life. In colonial America, you were apprenticed for six or more years to a master craftsman in order to learn the trade. You'd eat, drink, live, and work with that person to learn all that they had learned. Life knowledge was passed on in the context of a relationship, the opening up of one life to another. But the idea goes back even further than that—all the way back to the Bible. As mentioned earlier in this book, Jethro mentored his son-in-law, Moses. Moses then mentored his successor, Joshua. The prophet Elijah invested in the prophet Elisha. Mary, the mother of Jesus, turned to her older cousin, Elizabeth, for help. One of the greatest models for mentoring can be found in the life of Jesus. He focused on 120 people and, from that, he singled out seventy for special training and attention. Then from the seventy, he poured himself into twelve men—his intimate circle of disciples. He had those twelve men shadow his every step—eating with them, traveling with them, teaching them, living with them. And then, as we already discussed, from among the twelve, three received particular intensive time: Peter, James, and John.

A good mentor will walk with you in life, be a true brother or sister, challenge your thinking and faith, caution you when appropriate, and share what he or she has learned that might help you. Today, it's easy to get knowledge—what's tough to get is *wisdom*. But wisdom is what you can get from another person's life through your relationship with him or her.[17]

So how do you enter into a mentoring relationship? Keep your eye out for someone whom you respect, who seems strong in an area where you would like to grow, and with whom you seem to have some chemistry. And then begin to develop that relationship and spend some time with that person. Over the course of that time, invest in learning all you can, asking questions and becoming something of a student of their life.

Don't be awkward about this. I see a generation of young people desperate for mentors and counselors, and a generation of older people eager to pour into the lives of the young. Yet the young feel the older don't care or don't have the time, and the older feel the young aren't interested in anything they might have to offer. So a young woman, desperate for an older woman to talk with about life, relationships, marriage, child rearing, or prayer, sits alone; and the older woman, rich with wisdom and maturity, insight and experience, also sits alone. All when both would like to be sitting together.

And need to.

Join Some Kind of Group

A third step you can take is to become involved in some form of small group within the larger group of your community, such as a small group Bible study, support group, or serving team.

Small groups can provide a powerful environment for spiritual growth. A small group is just that—a small group of people who get together to build relationships, often around the study of the Bible, or a serving opportunity as part of a serving team. Through that group, they encourage each other in the faith. They become the small community within the larger community where you can experience the challenge, encouragement, and support you need. And hopefully they are a set of Christian friends who can become a support group for your faith.

I remember, just a few years ago, I felt prompted to take note of a series of events that came my way in just a single week. It was a week like any other week, but for whatever reason it was as if God was saying, "Make note of this—remember this, don't lose sight of what connecting people to me and to each other can mean."

Here were the situations:

A young couple in our church had a baby but had little or no support from their families. Another young woman who had a husband and two young children was diagnosed with muscular dystrophy. Two sisters experienced the death of their father. And a young entrepreneur had to liquidate his business due to bankruptcy.

All in one week.

Now in most cases, those people would have had to face those situations alone. Many people don't have community. They don't have people doing life with them—spurring them on to find God, follow God, experience God, and walk with God, and to be God's hands and feet and heart toward them.

Here's what happened.

I knew the young couple well, and when I went to visit them in the hospital, they had more people in their hospital room than I have ever seen—fourteen when I was there. With food, champagne, and childcare provided, and meals mapped out that were going to be brought their way for two weeks.

The young woman who was diagnosed with muscular dystrophy received phone calls, visits, prayer, meals, and the raw emotional support she so desperately needed as she faced the frightening future of her illness. There were even people who were able to connect her with a network of specialists.

The two sisters were ambushed with people praying for them, supporting them, listening to them as they grieved, and making sure that everything was arranged so that they could go to the funeral. One person offered to buy their plane ticket and another offered to care for their children while they traveled home for the funeral.

And the young entrepreneur had people in the church pray for him, encourage him, help him look for work, and even offer him employment—walking with him through every step of his crisis.

The ones caring for them, in each and every case, were their small group or serving team. They were a community within the community, a family within the family.

A Word to the Relationally Challenged

I know that for many of you, relationships are difficult. Many of us have made the mistake of investing ourselves into relationships that have left us deeply wounded. We've been abandoned, taken advantage of, betrayed, or misunderstood. When that happened, we felt like someone took a knife, plunged it into our heart, and twisted it around.

Sometimes it feels like we go from relationship to relationship, and the pain happens over and over again. And the tendency is to harden ourselves, lock up our hearts, and throw away the key. Nobody gets in, because when they do it just means more pain. We can develop an attitude that says, "I will not be hurt again." Then we begin to go through our lives emotionally detached. People can get close, but not too close. While that may keep you from being hurt by people, it doesn't keep you from hurting. The only pain worse than being hurt through a relationship is the pain of isolation and loneliness that comes from shutting yourself off from relationships.

I know. I am a very relationally challenged person. Intimacy has never been an easy affair. Added to that is the fact that I'm a flaming introvert—I gain my emotional energy from being alone. So if anyone knows the difficulties of making this investment, it's me. I have to *constantly* work at it. But I am going to be in strategic relationships with people through mentoring and small groups or serving teams for the rest of my life. Not because it's easy for me, and not because I always want to, but because it's *critical* for the life I want to live—and it's critical for yours too.

REFLECTION QUESTIONS

1. Have you experienced the new community yet through a church reflecting the four marks of true community? If so,

what are you doing right now to invest in that community? If not, what steps do you need to take to find one?

2. Who are the people fulfilling the role of the "one anothers" for you?

3. What person is a good example to you of how the Christian life should be lived?

4. Who is a VIP to you, who mentors you and ignites your love for God?

5. Where are you most susceptible to your VDPs, those who weaken and drain you?

6. What do you think would help strengthen your relationships?

CHAPTER SIX

WORSHIPING IN SPIRIT AND TRUTH

We worship our work, work at our play, and
play at our worship. —Leland Ryken[1]

I'll never forget the summer my family and I went to Washington, DC, and visited Arlington National Cemetery.

The first soldier, from the Civil War, was buried there in 1864. By the end of that year, more than seven thousand soldiers were laid to rest in its soil. Even those who had died before its establishment began to be moved to its hallowed grounds. As a result, the cemetery has become the burial ground for casualties from all of America's wars—from the Revolutionary War to the most recent of conflicts. More than four hundred thousand servicemen and -women are now buried on its 612 acres.

Beyond the thousands of white crosses dotting the landscape and marking the graves, we saw the burial sites of countless historical figures, including President Taft and Supreme Court Justices Oliver Wendell Holmes and Thurgood Marshall. There was the memorial to the crew of the space shuttle Challenger. We were moved by the flame that always burns at the site of President John F. Kennedy's grave, and the nearby site of his brother, Bobby. But nothing prepared us for the Tomb of the Unknown Soldier.

Established in 1921 as a burial place for the Unknown Soldier of World War I, unknown soldiers from World War II and the Korean War were soon added. An unknown soldier from the Vietnam War was buried there with full military honors on Memorial Day in 1984. The tomb itself simply says, "Here rests in honored glory an American soldier known but to God." In honor of all of those who died in combat defending our freedoms, there is a round-the-clock guard at the site of the tomb. A sentinel from the Third US Infantry maintains the vigil around the clock. In a symbolic mirroring of the 21-gun salute, the guard paces twenty-one steps down the mat before the tomb, pauses for twenty-one seconds, and returns. The changing of the guard takes place every hour, twenty-four hours a day, 365 days a year, rain or shine.

When we were there, it was packed with tourists, but you could have heard a pin drop. The sacred nature of what the place stood for, the solemn nature of the guard, the setting of the cemetery itself, lent itself to something that felt sacred, something that deserved honor and respect. No matter who you were or where you were from, it was natural, it was good, and it was right.

The word worship *comes from an old Anglo-Saxon word that literally read "worth-ship"—to give worth or honor to someone or something.*

It's right for God too.

Worship is when we collectively recognize the presence of God, giving him what he deserves, which is honor and respect, praise and devotion. There should be an outpouring of tribute and veneration, applause and acclaim. There should be worship.

That word can be like a strange taste on our palates. First, because it is mystical and almost surreal in nature. Also, because we just aren't into worshiping things. It seems primitive or beneath us. But there's still something about it that draws us in. Something about turning our inner selves toward another in awe and reverence that attracts us. Like the Tomb of the Unknown Soldier at Arlington.

We founded our country on the rejection of royalty and kings and monarchs—the rejection of all the pomp and circumstance, the kneeling and bowing. Yet we find ourselves fascinated by the lives and circumstances, ritual, and ceremony of the royal families that still survive in Europe. It's as if deep down we want there to be a sense of royalty somewhere in the world. Something magical, mythical, and grand that we can look to in awe and wonder.

The word *worship* comes from an old Anglo-Saxon word that literally read "worth-ship"—to give worth or honor to someone or something. According to the Bible, we were made for worship, and as Augustine explained so long ago, our hearts are restless until they have found the object of worship that we were created to honor. We are not truly complete until we have oriented our lives around that which we were created to hold in awe, wonder, and majesty.

It's the heart of our spiritual life.

What Makes Worship So Important

Until you become a worshiper of the One who is worthy of worship—the One who created you, formed you, and called you into being—you will never experience the spiritual depth and vitality that you were designed for. In fact, of all the spiritual investments that can be made, this may be the deepest, most personal, most life-changing investment of all. Yet it may also be the one people understand the least—and certainly *do* the least. As Leland Ryken once put it, our tendency is to "worship our work, work at our play, and play at our worship."[2] But playing at worship will cause us to miss out on all that worship can bring to our life, beginning with its role in helping us order our lives around God.

Worship Helps You Order Your Life around God

It is an old story, but it has always stuck with me. A radio broad-caster said that a man wrote in to his station asking him to sound the musical pitch A on his morning show. He said that he was a shepherd out on a remote ranch, far away from a piano. His only comfort was his old violin, and it was completely out of tune. The radio host agreed, sounded the tone on his show, and then received a short note that simply read, "Thanks. Now I am in tune." A simple little story, but it reminds me what worship can be in our lives—a clear, solid note that allows us to retune our lives to God. Gathering with others to bring all of our energies and senses to bear on the honor of God brings our lives into alignment with the heart of our spirituality. As Richard Foster has noted, "If worship does not change us, it has not been worship."[3] We can be seduced into thinking that all there is to living is the horizontal element—worship reminds us that there is a vertical element. Nothing else does that in our life; it's a powerful immersion that forces us to look up while kneeling down.

Worship Helps You Encounter and Experience God

A second reason worship is so vital to our spiritual lives is that it helps us encounter and experience God. No one wants dead, lifeless ritual. We don't want dried-out dogma. We don't want meaningless symbols and prac-tices. We want to *engage* God, to *experience* God. God wants that for us too. And he's de-signed the way for it to happen: worship. Jesus promised that "where two or three gather in my name, there am I with them" (Matt. 18:20).

"Where two or three gather in my name, there am I with them" (Matt. 18:20).

God is present in the gathered community of worship in a way unlike any other moment. And his presence is there for *encounter*.

Worship Helps You Respond to God

A third benefit of worship for your life is that it helps you respond to God. When you love someone, it's natural to want to let those feelings be known. You want to *tell* them, *show* them, *do something* for them.

Worship is one of the most personal, sincere, authentic ways to respond to God relationally. When you articulate your feelings, expressing yourself verbally and emotionally and physically, it deepens your relationship with God. I can't imagine being in a growing, intimate relationship with my wife without regularly telling her how I feel about her, how much I care about her, that she's important to me, and that I love her. This is why the Bible presents worship in terms of expression, such as in the seventy-first psalm: "I will praise you with music, telling of your faithfulness to all your promises. . . . I will . . . sing your praises for redeeming me. I will talk to others all day long about your justice and your goodness" (vv. 22–24 TLB). And in Psalm 59, David, the king of Israel, said, "I will sing about your power. Each morning I will sing with joy about your unfailing love. For you have been my refuge, a place of safety when I am in distress. . . . To you I sing praises, . . . the God who shows me unfailing love" (vv. 16–17 NLT). I know that many people have a hard time expressing their feelings to other people, much less God. But even the most awkward attempts at expressing that love matter.

Worship Helps You Celebrate God

A fourth payoff is that worship helps you celebrate God. To celebrate God is to take time to remember all that he's done and say, "Yea, God!" It's like having a party in his honor. Take a look at the spirit of this through the ninety-sixth psalm in the Bible:

> Sing GOD a brand-new song!
> Earth and everyone in it, sing!
> Sing to GOD—worship GOD! . . .

For GOD is great, and worth a thousand Hallelujahs. . . .

Bravo, GOD, Bravo!
Everyone join in the great shout: Encore!
In awe before the beauty, in awe before the might.

Bring gifts and celebrate,
. . . everyone worship!

Get out the message—GOD Rules! . . .

Let's hear it from Sky,
With Earth joining in,
And a huge round of applause from Sea.

Let Wilderness turn cartwheels,
Animals, come dance,
Put every tree of the forest in the choir—

An extravaganza before GOD as he comes.
   (vv. 1–2, 4, 7–13 MSG)

Now that's a party! We need to take time to do that. We need to stop and applaud and cheer. Any good leader will tell you of the importance of taking time as a team to *celebrate*. If teams don't hit the pause button in the midst of the push and pull of what they are trying to accomplish together to remember all that has been accomplished so far, then they can lose their passion and vision for the ongoing demands of the task. It's important to stop and say, "You know, it's been a good season. Let's just stop and celebrate." As important as that is organizationally, it's even more important *spiritually*.

The Bible says that every good and perfect gift is from God. Everything good, everything noble, everything praiseworthy, everything that has worth and merit and truth and goodness is from him. What moves your spiritual life from one that is lifeless to one that is passionate is to practice the celebration of the goodness of God. You are meant to celebrate all that he is, all that he has done, and all that he is doing in you, with you, and through you.

Worship Helps You Receive Spiritual Encouragement and Energy

Finally, worship helps you receive spiritual encouragement and energy. Recall these verses we looked at earlier from the book of Hebrews: "Let us consider how we may spur one another on toward love and good deeds, not giving up meeting together, as some are in the habit of doing, but encouraging one another" (10:24–25). While the primary purpose of worship is not what we get out of it, but what we give to God *through* it, when you gather together with others to worship, there's no way you can walk away without receiving an injection of spiritual energy and encouragement.

> "Let us consider how we may spur one another on toward love and good deeds, not giving up meeting together, as some are in the habit of doing, but encouraging one another" (Heb. 10:24–25).

For all these reasons and more, worship has marked Christians from the very beginning and was at the heart of the pulsating energy of the early church: "They devoted themselves . . . to the breaking of bread and to prayer. . . . Every day they continued to meet together in the temple courts. They broke bread in their homes and ate together with glad and sincere hearts, praising God" (Acts 2:42, 46–47). When it says that they devoted themselves to the breaking of bread and to prayer, and that they met in the temple courts, that means they were gathering together for times of communal worship, including the celebration of the Lord's Supper, or communion. This wasn't just a group of religious people attending weekly services. These were authentic worshipers who were worshiping as a natural, almost impromptu response to what God was doing in their lives. Luke, who captured that picture of the early church in Acts, talks about them doing it with certain kinds of hearts, and with an intense and purposeful level of activity. They were more like raving fans at a football game choosing to show up for their team or spilling out onto the streets for a celebratory parade than passive participants in some kind of stuffy, lifeless ritual or routine. Worship was a tangible reaction erupting in their life in response to a living and active God who had rocked their world.

I'll never forget traveling to Urbana, Illinois, when I was in college for a huge gathering of university students. More than seventeen thousand of us had crammed into an auditorium on the campus of the University of Illinois at Champaign-Urbana on New Year's Eve for a worship celebration. What we didn't know was that the top of the auditorium had become covered with huge sheets of ice. As we sang, pouring out our hearts in celebration of God, vibrations from our voices began to shake the ice loose. So as we were singing, we could hear huge sheets of ice sliding off the top of the auditorium, serving as a thunderous echo to our offering to God. Joining voices with thousands of other people, hearing the rumble of ice coming off the building as we sang, and then, at midnight, taking communion together to usher in the new year was simply one of the most remarkable shots of spiritual adrenaline I've ever experienced. But I shouldn't have been surprised. That's the nature of worship.

How to Worship

So how do you do it? Is worship simply attending a service and singing a song? Not according to Jesus. Here's what he had to say: "True worshipers will worship the Father in spirit and in truth. The Father is looking for those who will worship him that way. For God is Spirit, so those who worship him must worship in spirit and in truth" (John 4:23–24 NLT). When it comes to worship, Jesus taught two things: that we should worship God in *spirit* and in *truth*. Let's start off with truth.

Worshiping God in Truth

To worship in truth means that when we worship God, we worship God as he *really is*, not some false idea of God or some substitute for God. True Christian worship rests not only on the *act* of worship, but on the *object* of worship. To worship in truth means to worship the only true object for worship—God. There are many other objects you could choose to worship—money, fame, a rock, a tree, even a distorted view of God—but that wouldn't be the worship you were created for, much less a worship that would do anything for your life. Because only worship in truth—the worship of the one, true God as revealed in Scripture—is really worship.

> "True worshipers will worship the Father in spirit and in truth. The Father is looking for those who will worship him that way. For God is Spirit, so those who worship him must worship in spirit and in truth" (John 4:23–24 NLT).

There must be a conscious, intelligent, theological dynamic to worship. It is not simply an emotional or experiential event, but a cerebral one. You are thinking as you worship, and those must be right thoughts. You worship when you are thinking rightly about God and your relationship with God.

Worshiping God in Spirit

Jesus also said to worship in spirit. To worship in spirit is to worship authentically with your *heart*, to have your act of worship be sincere, genuine, and real. Jesus said it's not just *whom* you worship that matters but also *how* you worship.

There's an old story I once heard about a man who went to church with an angel as his guide. Every seat in the sanctuary was filled, but there was something strange about the service. The organist moved her fingers over the keys, but no music came from its pipes. The choir rose to sing and their lips moved, but not a sound was to be heard. The pastor stepped to the pulpit to read the Scriptures, but the man with the angel could not even detect the rustle of the pages. The Lord's Prayer was recited by the entire congregation, but not a single syllable was audible. The pastor again went to the pulpit, and the man watched as the minister gestured here and there to make his various points, but he heard nothing.

Turning to the angel, the man said, "I don't understand. What does all of this mean? I see that a service is being held, but I hear nothing."

The angel replied, "You hear nothing because there is nothing to be heard. You see the service as God sees it. These people honor him with their lips, but their hearts are far from him. Worship without the heart is not worship."

Ways to Worship

So we are to worship in spirit and truth. That's easy enough to understand. But what are some of the ways of actually doing that?

Music

One of the most common and most significant ways to worship God is through music. There are forty-one different psalms in the Bible that encourage us to sing to God. There's something about music that moves us and lets us express ourselves in powerful and meaningful ways. To use music to worship God, we take the words to the song and make them *our* words. We use them as a vehicle to express how *we* feel and what *we* want to say. As Psalm 100 says, "Sing yourselves into his presence" (v. 2 MSG).

Body

A second way you can worship is through your *body*. Look at this sampling from the Bible:

> I lift up my hands
>> toward your Most Holy Place. (Ps. 28:2)

> I spread out my hands to you. (Ps. 88:9)

The people all stood up. . . . All the people lifted their hands and responded, "Amen! Amen!" Then they bowed down and worshiped the LORD with their faces to the ground. (Neh. 8:5–6)

We are physical creatures, and we tend to express ourselves physically. Let's say the quarterback of your favorite team connects to the tight end for a touchdown to win the game. Do you just sit there and yawn? No! You jump up and scream at the top of your lungs, clap and shout, hug the person next to you, and pump your fist in the air. The more comfortable you become with worship, the more comfortable you become expressing yourself physically to God in ways that seem natural and appropriate to who you are and how you're feeling. I don't mean you do an end-zone dance—when it comes to worship, you should never act in a way that draws attention to yourself and away from God—but when you worship, you might want to kneel, clap, or close your eyes and just soak it all in; you might want to raise your hands as a symbol of praise. Your body is part of who you are and is often essential to expressing yourself in worship to God.

Acts and Events

A third way we can worship is through certain acts or events. In the Bible, taking up an offering is considered an act of worship. Praying can be an act of worship. Reading or reciting Scripture can be an act of worship. Dance, drama, and film can all facilitate worship. But there are two acts of worship that deserve special attention. One is a solitary, one-time event, while the other is to be an ongoing investment. The single event is baptism, and the continued practice is the celebration of communion, also known as the Eucharist (a word for "thankfulness") or the Lord's Supper. Both are "command performances" for your spiritual life, which is why they are deemed sacraments. Let's begin with baptism.

Christian Baptism

Jesus was baptized, and he taught that everyone who chooses to follow him should be baptized as well. In one of the most famous passages in the Bible, known as the Great Commission, Jesus said, "Therefore, go and make disciples of all the nations, baptizing them in the name of the Father and the Son and the Holy Spirit" (Matt. 28:19 NLT). This makes baptism one of the clearest demonstrations that you really are a Christian. The Bible even says that "we know that we have come to know him if we keep his commands" (1 John 2:3).

So what is the meaning of baptism? First and foremost, it illustrates Christ's death, burial, and resurrection. The Bible says, "For when you were baptized, you were buried with Christ, and in baptism you were also raised with Christ" (Col. 2:12 GNT).

Baptism is like a wedding ring—it's the outward sign of the commitment you have made within your heart.

Baptism also illustrates your new life as a Christian. Notice how this is expressed in the Bible: "By our baptism, then, we were buried with him and shared his death, in order that, just as Christ was raised from death . . . so also we might live a new life" (Rom. 6:4 GNT). To this point, in the very early life of the ancient church, when people emerged from the baptismal waters they would be clothed with a white robe to symbolize their new life in Christ, free from the stain of sin. Yet baptism doesn't make you a Christian. Only your faith in Christ does that. Baptism is like a wedding ring—it's the outward sign of the commitment you have made within your heart.

Most people are aware that there are differences in the way churches baptize people. Some do it by immersion, others by sprinkling. Many have concluded that immersion is most in line with the biblical evidence, not to mention the spirit of the symbol as it relates to Christ's burial and resurrection.[4] It seems to be the way Jesus himself was baptized, and every other baptism recorded in the Bible was by immersion.[5] The word *baptizo* is a transliteration from the Greek alphabet and where we get our word *baptize* that means to dip, plunge, or immerse under water.[6] But the *method* of baptism is not as important as the *act* of baptism. Every person who becomes a Christian should be baptized as a Christian. In the Bible, we find a close connection between decision and public profession of faith. For example, the book of Acts records, "Many of them believed . . . were baptized . . . that day" (2:41 GNT). And when Philip led an Ethiopian man, a eunuch and high official in his native land, to Christ, the man said,

> "Look, here is water. What can stand in the way of my being baptized?" Philip said, "If you believe with all your heart, you may." The eunuch answered, "I believe that Jesus Christ is the Son of God." . . . Then both Philip and the eunuch went down into the water and Philip baptized him. (Acts 8:36–38)

But this does not mean that baptism has to follow immediately after salvation. What the Bible is trying to teach is that baptism should follow your decision to become a believer, not come before. Also, that there is no reason to delay. If you wait until you are "good" enough, you will never feel ready for baptism.

If you were baptized as an infant, then it is likely your faith tradition has some form of confirmation process that should be followed with sincere conviction, else the purpose and meaning of your baptism was lost. The purpose of baptism is to confess your personal commitment to Christ publicly; regardless of method, this purpose must not be lost. If you have not been baptized, or if an earlier event failed to represent a true declaration of faith, you should pursue Christian baptism as a believer.[7]

The Lord's Supper

The second act of worship commanded by Jesus was to remember his death through the taking of bread and wine. Unlike the once-for-all nature of Christian baptism, the Lord's Supper is to be repeated with frequency in our lives as an active memorial.

The background for the Lord's Supper is the Jewish Passover festival, which marked how the Jewish people had been liberated from Egyptian bondage through the plagues God brought on Egypt through Moses. The tenth and decisive plague was the death of the firstborn of Egypt. The sacrifice of an animal was a common way for people of that culture to atone for their sins, and God told the Israelites that if they would sacrifice an unblemished lamb—one without a defect—and then take that blood and spread it on their doorposts, the angel of death would pass over them and not take the life of their firstborn: hence the term *Passover*.

People put the blood on the doorposts, the angel came, the firstborn of Egypt were killed, but the Israelites were passed over. This had such an impact on the leaders of Egypt that they released the Israelites from bondage. Jewish people have been celebrating the festival of Passover ever since as a reminder of God's deliverance from death and the freedom that came from that deliverance through the blood of a lamb.

As the festival developed, it came to include a lamb that was slaughtered and eaten, along with unleavened bread and bitter herbs as a reminder that their departure from Egypt was so hurried that they were unable to add yeast. Even more importantly, the bitter taste of the herbs was a reminder of the bitterness of the bondage from which they had been released. A cup of wine was always set aside for the Messiah, but never drunk, in case he came that very night to bring deliverance. The Passover was always to be celebrated as a family, to remind the Israelites that they were saved as a community and called out of bondage as a community, in order to be a community.[8]

Just before his death, Jesus gathered his disciples together to celebrate the Passover, but with a twist. He said that now this wine and bread would have a new meaning. From now on, the meal would represent *him* as the unblemished lamb that was sacrificed. And those who would be marked by *his* blood would be freed from the bondage of their sin and would be passed over from the spiritual death that comes from sin.

Jesus said from now on, Christians should "do this in remembrance of me" (Luke 22:19). The Lord's Supper is the *new* memorial meal for those who are part of the family of God. The bread is eaten in remembrance of his body, broken for us; the wine as a symbol of his blood, shed on the cross. And the cup set aside for the Messiah is now raised to our lips—for the Messiah, in the person of Jesus, has come. Jesus was the true sacrificial lamb for the Passover; his death now serves as the ultimate and final deliverance of God's people from their sins.

This is why Paul writes in his letter to the church at Corinth that "Christ, our Passover lamb, has been sacrificed" (1 Cor. 5:7). The church has been celebrating the Lord's Supper ever since as a family of faith.

But while it's a time of remembrance, the Lord's Supper is far from being a time of mere recollection. The Greek word Jesus used for *remembrance* is best understood as an affectionate calling of the person to mind, a reliving of a past event. Jesus wanted this meal to be a remembrance that would transport what was buried in the past to a dynamic place in the present. So through the celebration of the Supper we remember Christ's death, our acceptance of his death on our behalf, our

> *Jesus wanted this meal to be a remembrance that would transport what was buried in the past to a dynamic place in the present.*

promise at baptism to lead a new life, and the spiritual strength and blessing that God has given—and will give us—for our spiritual journey. It is the high point of Christian worship.

I mentioned earlier that I served as a professor at the Moscow Theological Institute. One night a group of us went to the famed Bolshoi Ballet. It was a long, wonderful evening, but after we took the subway back to where we were staying, the students said, "Come and let us celebrate." The other two professors with me were as tired as I was, but the students were so intent on our joining them that we went. Then we found out what celebration meant to them. They wanted to gather in the dining room and sing hymns and worship God. And we did, late into the night, with more passion and sincerity than I have ever experienced. It didn't matter that we didn't sing in Russian—we worshiped God together.

But I went to bed puzzled. I had never seen such passion for spontaneous and heart-filled worship. I was curious as to why they were so ready and eager to offer God love and honor. I received my answer the following Sunday when I was invited to speak at a church in North Moscow. A former underground church that met in secret, as so many churches had been, they were now meeting openly in a schoolhouse. I had been asked to bring a message that Sunday morning. I didn't know that I was in for a bit of a wait.

The service lasted for nearly three hours. There were three sermons from three different speakers, with long periods of worship between each message. I was to go last. When the service was over, I talked a bit with the pastor of the church. I was surprised at not only the length of the service, but the spirit and energy of the people. During the entire three hours, they never let up. Throughout the service, they never seemed to tire. Even at the end, they didn't seem to want to go home.

"In the States," I said, "you're doing well to go a single hour before every watch in the place starts beeping." (This was before the time of cell phones, mind you.) He didn't get my weak attempt at humor, but he did say something that I will never forget.

"It was only a few years ago that we would have been put in prison for doing what we did today. We were never allowed to gather together as a community of faith and offer worship to God. We are just so happy, and almost in a state of unbelief, that we can do this now—publicly, together—that we don't want it to end. And not knowing what the future might hold for us here, we assume that every week might just be our last. So we don't ever want to stop. So we keep worshiping together, as long as we can."

As I left, his words never left my mind. And I thought, *I will never think about worship the same again. I've been too casual about it, too laid-back, taken it too much for granted. These people know what it's about—really about—and because of that, they have been willing, and would be willing again, to suffer for it. To be imprisoned for it. To die for it. They've discovered that true worship has a high yield for their lives. The simple act of worship has that much meaning and significance to them. It matters that much.*

I thought, *And it should matter that much to me.*

REFLECTION QUESTIONS

1. What does it mean to worship God in truth?

2. How can a person worship God in spirit?

3. Each person has unique talents and different modes of expression. What form of worship comes easiest to you (e.g., music, singing, giving, serving, praying, writing, etc.)?

4. How can someone begin to consider all of life as an act of worship?

CHAPTER SEVEN

BECOMING A PLAYER

There is more about you than meets the eye. — *Gandalf to Frodo*[1]

When you were young, what did you want to be when you grew up? When my oldest daughter, Rebecca, was only four, she informed my wife that when she grew up, she was going to be a farmer.

My wife said, "That's nice, dear."

"Yep," Rebecca continued, "when I grow up, I'm gonna be a farmer, and I'm gonna marry Daddy!"

Then Susan said, "But if you grow up and become a farmer, and marry Daddy, what will *Mommy* do?"

Rebecca pondered that seriously for a moment or two, then she brightened up and said, "You can be our cow!"

All of us have different dreams, different ideas of what we want our lives to be like. And for most of us, there is a common denominator: *We want to make a difference.* We want our lives to stand out and to count for something. We know we are players in a game, and we don't want to be sitting on the bench.

Why Serving Matters

Making a difference matters—not just in terms of personal fulfillment, but in regard to spiritual development. The heart of difference-making is the giving away of yourself, the investing of yourself. According to the math of the Christian life, the more you give, the more you receive. This is why Jesus was simultaneously the most influential figure in all of human history and the ultimate model of spiritual living. For he "did not come to be served, but to serve," and to give his life away (Mark 10:45). We too are called to be servants, and serving others is essential to our spiritual life. So how does this actually work? In four ways:

Serving Others Gets You into Spiritual Shape

First, serving others gets you into spiritual shape by putting you through a spiritual workout. When you serve, you build up your faith. Think about how it works with your body. When you lift weights, you increase the levels of contractile proteins and connective tissue in the muscles you exercise, making those muscles bigger than they were before. Your spiritual life works that way when it comes to serving, because it is through serving that you give your faith the necessary workout it needs to grow strong. If you're *not* serving, your spiritual life will be weak, flabby, and undeveloped.

Serving Others Gets You into the Game

A second benefit of serving is that it gets you into the game. It's the way you become a player and get involved in what God is doing in the world. This is one of our chief purposes in life, for the Bible says, "For we are God's masterpiece. He has created us anew in Christ Jesus, so we can do the good things he planned for us long ago" (Eph. 2:10 NLT). You were created to take who God made you to be and put yourself into play. Following that purpose will put more gas into your spiritual tank than you could possibly imagine. Think about it: Are you more passionate about something you're involved in than something you just watch from a distance? When you get off the sidelines and become a player for God, what God is doing becomes a lot more important to you.

Serving Others Lets You Make a Difference

The third payoff of serving others is one we've already explored: It enables you to make a difference in this world, to do something more than just make money, or put together a business deal, or buy a dream house, or take a vacation. We want our lives to count; we want to do something with our lives that will matter. And there's only one way for that to happen: to make the investment of service. Once you do, make no mistake, you will taste what making a difference is all about. All you have to do is see one changed life, hear one thank you, see one brief glimpse of impact from some act of service that you've done, and your life will never be the same. Because then you'll see things from a different vantage point—a little higher, a little more eternal. And you'll say, "Most of the things I've done with my life won't add up to much, but this, this will live on; this mattered; this made a difference."

> ▶ **WHY SERVING MATTERS**
>
> IT GETS YOU INTO SPIRITUAL SHAPE.
> IT GETS YOU INTO THE GAME.
> IT LETS YOU MAKE A DIFFERENCE.
> IT AMPLIFIES YOUR IMPACT.

Serving Others Amplifies Your Impact

Throughout his presidency of the United States, Ronald Reagan kept a sign on his desk that said, "It's amazing how much you can get done if you don't care who gets the credit." Making a difference does not always mean taking center stage. Serving enables something to take place because you supported it and helped make it happen. But this life of service to others is a high and challenging calling. Consider the following words by Ruth Harms Calkins:

You know, Lord, how I serve You
With great emotional fervor

In the limelight.
You know how eagerly I speak for You
At a women's club.
You know how I effervesce when I promote
A fellowship group.
You know my genuine enthusiasm
At a Bible study.
But how would I react, I wonder
If You pointed to a basin of water
And asked me to wash the calloused feet
Of a bent and wrinkled old woman
Day after day
Month after month
In a room where nobody saw
And nobody knew.[2]

Discover Your DNA

One of the most ambitious projects ever undertaken was known as the Human Genome Project. It was an international scientific research project with the goal of mapping out human DNA, which stands for deoxyribonucleic acid and is the basic material in the chromosomes of the cell nucleus. It contains your genetic code and transmits your hereditary pattern. From a physical standpoint, it is the makeup of who you are. It determines everything from the color of your hair to your height.

Launched in 1990, and completed thirteen years later in 2003, the Human Genome Project has been called the biological equivalent of the moon shot of the Apollo program. The benefits of this project have been incalculable, particularly with molecular medicine. The project has helped us understand diseases, including genotyping specific viruses, identification of mutations linked to various forms of cancer, and so much more. It's helped us understand ourselves.[3]

But that's only one kind of DNA.

There's another kind of DNA that flows through our veins—only this kind isn't physical. It's deeper than that. It's psychological, emotional, and spiritual. This kind of DNA, which is every bit as distinctive and representative for your life as your physical DNA, is who you are as a person.

Your SHAPE

Let's talk about this DNA in terms of your *shape*. Because you have one. A distinctive one. One that no one else on earth has. It was given to you by God himself. The Old Testament says this about God: "Your hands shaped me and made me" (Job 10:8). And then later, it records these words from God through the prophet Isaiah: "The people I have shaped for myself will broadcast my praises" (Isa. 43:21 NJB). Do you know your shape? Do you know who you really are? Your makeup? Your design? Who it is that God has made you to be? Until you do, there's no way to know how to follow your purpose, because your purpose in life is connected to your shape. You're made the way you are for a reason.

So what's your shape? This is an acrostic I borrowed from a friend that pulls together the Bible's teaching on this in a helpful way.[4]

Spiritual gifts
Heart
Abilities
Personality
Experience

Spiritual Gifts

The acrostic begins with the letter *S* for *spiritual gifts*. You may have never heard that phrase—spiritual gifts—before, but it's a very important idea in the Bible. When you become a Christian, the Bible says that the Holy Spirit takes up residence in your life. One of the things he does is give you at least one spiritual gift—usually more.

A spiritual gift is a supernatural ability to develop a particular capability for the cause of Christ.

So what's a spiritual gift? Here is the simplest definition I know: A spiritual gift is a supernatural *ability* to develop a particular *capability* for the cause of Christ. It's some area or some way that God makes you a "10" or with the potential to be a "10." Here's how the Bible talks about it:

> Now, . . . regarding your question about the special abilities the Spirit gives us. . . . There are different kinds of spiritual gifts, but the same Spirit is the source of them all. There are different kinds of service, but we serve the same Lord. God works in different ways, but it is the same God who does the work in all of us. A spiritual gift is given to each of us so we can help each other. (1 Cor. 12:1, 4–7 NLT)

Here's another taste of the Bible's teaching: "Christ has given each of us special abilities—whatever he wants us to have out of his rich storehouse of gifts" (Eph. 4:7 TLB). Spiritual gifts are special capabilities that God gives to us when we enter into a relationship with him as followers of Christ. They are direct enablements by God to do something that bears the stamp of his power. It's the touch of God *on* a life, and the work of God *through* a life. It's something we are enabled to do through which God shows up and gives us disproportionate impact and influence.

There are four different lists of spiritual gifts in the New Testament, each varying from the other.[5] The idea seems to be that the lists are indicative, not exhaustive, and that the number of spiritual gifts is limited only by the will and desire of the Holy Spirit. This means there are all kinds of gifts. There are administrative gifts, teaching gifts, gifts of hospitality, giving, wisdom, discernment.

There are gifts related to encouragement and mercy. There are gifts related to raw creativity in an area, a particular skill set related to computers, business, mechanics, or cooking. It may be the ability to communicate spiritual truths and answer questions. It may be answering the phone or greeting in a way that puts someone at ease, makes them feel valued and want to take a step forward. It could be the ability to bring healing to another person through the gifts of counseling, medicine, or even prayer. It may be in the realm of the arts—dancing, singing, acting, playing an instrument, videography. It may be investing in the educational system or the judicial system or taking up a role in the media. It could be loving and serving fifth graders in a way they have never been loved and served before. It may be the gift of leadership: the ability to engender followers and cast vision, catalyze resources, and advance a cause.

The list goes on and on. Spiritual gifts are limited only by the creativity of the Holy Spirit who gives these gifts. No gift is better or more spiritual than another. They are all special, because whatever gift you possess was handpicked and given to you, personally, by God. This makes spiritual gifts one of those exciting, mystical, mysterious places where the divine mingles with the human. Where God expresses himself in a life. Your area of gifting bristles with God's energy, and when you put your gift into play, God shows up in ways that are unmistakable.

If you are a Christ follower, you have at least one of these. No matter who you are. It was given to you the moment you gave your life to Christ. I cannot stress enough how important it is to get in touch with the spiritual gifts you have been given. The God of the universe—who willed you into existence—handpicked, handcrafted, wrapped up, and put your name on the outside of a gift that he has given you. A gift that was designed so you could both find and follow your purpose in life and make your mark on this world. Discovering your gift is integral to finding your purpose in life and learning how you are intended to make a difference with your life. Do you know your top giftings? There are any number of spiritual gift assessments you can take to help you on this journey. Take one.[6] When you take one of those assessments you will see there's usually a cluster of gifts where you rank high, a cluster where you rank low, and then some in the middle that don't rank particularly high or low. But take the time to find out.

Heart

The *H* in SHAPE stands for *heart*. Your heart has to do with your passions. Your passions are your interests, your loves, what you care about, what you follow online, what puts gas in your tank, what you enjoy doing. But don't reduce this to a hobby, your latest binge on Netflix, or a favorite sports team. That would be superficial. A passion is what captivates you, motivates you, and stirs you most deeply. It can be anything: technology, education, science, children, politics, economics, or sports. What transforms an interest into a passion is when something drives you to want to act. So it's not just a heart for children, it's wanting to serve homeless boys at their most vulnerable season of life. It's not just being interested in sports but wanting to use soccer to reach out to atheist kids in Eastern Europe. It's not just taking an interest in education but wanting to stamp out illiteracy.

So what is it that captivates your conscience, grips your spirit, and exercises your emotions? What areas, what concerns, grab hold of you? What energizes you when you study it or think about it? What kind of articles, online blogs, or news stories stick with you and occupy your thoughts? Whether it's about the need for foster parents, the opioid epidemic, young kids being exposed to porn, gun violence, the need for fathers to step up and lead—no matter what it is, get in touch with your God-given passion.

If you genuinely don't think you have a passion for anything, ask God to give you one. Because what we're really talking about is your heart. Your heart was made by God, is stirred by God and, if you'll let him, can be directed by God. So ask him to reveal your passions to you. The Bible says, "Watch over your heart; *that's* where life starts" (Prov. 4:23 MSG, italics in original). Passion is what stirs the deepest part of who you are in a way that propels you into action or concern.

Getting in touch with your passion is a God thing, because it's part of who God created you to be. So ask yourself some questions: What gets you excited? What are you enthusiastic about? What touches your emotions most deeply? What stirs you to want to take action? You have an emotional heartbeat. Listen to it.

Abilities

The next letter in the word SHAPE is *A*, which stands for your *abilities*—those natural talents and skills that you were born with. Those are a God thing too. Here's how simply the Bible puts it: "God has given each of us the ability to do certain things well" (Rom. 12:6 TLB). The difference between a natural ability or talent and a spiritual gift is that a natural talent is just that—natural. It's not *super*natural, coming to you later as a gift from God that results from your relationship with him.

Natural gifts and abilities are usually with you from day one. For example, I've heard people talk about how you can spot a natural leader on the playground a mile away. Three or four kids are on the playground, and one says, "Let's play football." A couple of them say, "Okay, let's go." But then Bobby says, "Nah, I don't want to. You guys can go on. I'm going to play basketball." So he does, and he's willing to go off on his own and do that. But when Bobby does that, instead of playing football the others decide they want to play basketball too. They want to do what Bobby wants to do. Why? Bobby is just a natural leader. He goes off in a direction, and when he looks over his shoulder, people are following him. That natural leadership ability of Bobby's will be with him the rest of his life. It's how God wired him.

One interesting dynamic is how often God will take a natural gift or ability in someone and then, once they become a Christ follower, infuse that natural ability with supernatural giftedness and turn it into a spiritual gift. So what natural abilities has God given you? Is it teaching? Leadership? Creativity in the arts? Are you skilled at counseling, coaching, or team building? You probably know of at least one area where you're pretty good at something. This ability has been affirmed, because you've seen success. That's part of your God-given SHAPE.

One word of advice: make sure you don't dismiss too quickly what may or may not be a true natural ability. Let God and those closest to you—and the test of time—be the judge. A schoolteacher once told a seven-year-old boy he should drop out of school because he wasn't inventive. That boy was Thomas Edison, who invented, among many other things, the light bulb, the telephone, and the phonograph. Someone else told Mozart that his music had too many notes and no one would ever like it. Another told Rembrandt that his paintings would never be remembered. Another boy was told he was a poor student, especially in mathematics. Diagnosed as mentally slow, there was an effort to remove him from school. Good thing they let Einstein stay. The author of *Gone with the Wind* was rejected by major publishers for years. The Decca recording company told the Beatles they didn't like their sound, because groups with guitars were on their way out. Walt Disney's first job was at a newspaper, and the editor told him he had—get this—no creativity.[7] When you evaluate your abilities, make sure you don't brush aside those tied to a passion too quickly just because someone else doesn't see in you what God may have very well placed there.

Personality

Another aspect of your God-given shape is your *personality*. That's what the letter *P* in SHAPE stands for. Every one of us has a unique inner world, a specific internal makeup and disposition. This is one of the meanings within the words of Psalm 139, which says, "For you [God] created my inmost being" (v. 13). Your "inmost being" is who you are, your personality, your consciousness— what makes you *you*. No one personality type is better or worse than another. This is what the apostle Paul was after when he wrote in 1 Corinthians that "God works through different [people] in different ways, but it is the same God who achieves his purpose through them all" (12:6 Phillips). Your personality is precious and unique, and it is just as God-given and God-fashioned as the color of your eyes.

Many of us have taken the Myers-Briggs test, probably the most famous of all the personality tests. We talk about being ENTJs or INTJs, INFPs or ENTPs. On the Myers-Briggs I am an INTJ. That stands for introvert, intuitive, thinking, judging. I can't begin to tell you how important it was for me to get in touch with the first of those four letters—being an introvert.

I honestly didn't know that's what I was for a long time. People assumed—and I assumed too—I was extroverted because I was good with people, comfortable in up-front roles and public speaking, and found myself in leadership positions. But I wasn't an extrovert. The truth is that I got all of my emotional energy from being alone. Too much people-time in a given day and I would end up in a fetal position. And I wouldn't know why! But now I do. I love people, but I get my emotional energy away from people. Knowing that has helped me immensely.

What's your personality type? Do you know? You should.

Experience

The last letter in SHAPE is *E* and stands for your *experiences*: your experiences in terms of knowledge, wisdom, background, and education that you have stored up throughout your life. It's as if everything you've ever done, everything you've ever gone through, has made a deposit in your experience bank. Those deposits were made for a reason. God gives us a unique, personal experience account to draw from.

I have a son-in-law who is a physician. When he was preparing his application for his residency, he had to write an essay about why he became a doctor. He sent it to me to look over. He wrote something in that essay that I didn't know before. He said he could trace his pursuit of medicine all the way back to when he was a boy. He took a first-aid class right before attending a summer camp where someone became injured. No one knew what to do; he was the only one on the scene who had even the most rudimentary knowledge. He jumped in and was able to serve in a strategic way. That event, and the feeling of serving in that way, marked him. He loved treating that physical need; he loved being a calming presence in the midst of anxiety. It led him to a premed track in college, to medical school, residency, to a fellowship in internal medicine, and now to a practice where he specializes in gastrointestinal medicine.

All because of an experience.

We all have them. But are we listening to them? The Bible records Moses saying, "Remember today what you have learned about the LORD through your experiences with him" (Deut. 11:2 GNT). And in the New Testament, Paul challenged people this way: "Were all your experiences wasted? I hope not!" (Gal. 3:4 NCV). And in another letter, Paul added this: "We know that all that happens to us is working for our good if we love God and are fitting into his plans" (Rom. 8:28 TLB). This doesn't mean that all experiences are good, but it does mean that all experiences can work for good. Even the most painful things. Henri Nouwen once wrote about the idea that asking what has wounded you is like asking what has made you.[8] So walk through your past experiences and think about your family of origin (good and bad), education, vocational experiences, spiritual background—but don't forget the dark, hard, traumatic times. They are all part of your SHAPE.

Do What You Are

Of course, just knowing about your SHAPE and getting in touch with it is not the point. The point is to do what you are! You may have been taught that you are what you do. That's not the way it's supposed to be. The truth is that you should *do* what you *are*.

Jim Collins, arguably one of the best writers and thinkers currently in regard to business, wrote a book titled *Good to Great*. The idea was to investigate businesses that started out at best "good," but then went on to be "great." What enabled them to do that? One of the ideas Collins explored was called the "Hedgehog Concept."[9] It's based on the idea that there are two types of companies in the world: hedgehogs and foxes. Foxes chase after all kinds of things at the same time, running around after anything and everything. They have no sense of purpose, no sense of direction, but lots of activity.

Hedgehogs, on the other hand, go after one main thing and stay focused on true north. The research of Collins found that hedgehogs outpace foxes. The companies that make the biggest impact are hedgehogs. Here's how the great companies found their hedgehog—their one big idea or pursuit in life. It was based on three circles:

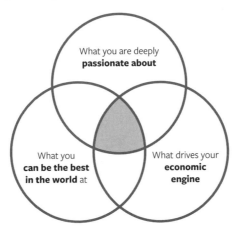

The first circle is what you are deeply passionate about. The second circle is what drives your economic engine. It's asking, "What can we do that we can monetize?" The third circle is what you can be the best in the world at—and, just as important, what you can *never* be the best in the world at. Where these three circles overlap is the company's hedgehog concept—their sweet spot, their purpose, their pursuit—the one big thing they should focus on.

When that book came out, it was used by a lot of teams, a lot of companies, even a lot of churches. They gathered people together to go through the book and determine their hedgehog concept. What I found interesting was that so many people reading it soon stopped reflecting on it as merely a business or company book. They began to read it *personally*. Teams would go through it for corporate reasons, but people were reading it for themselves. They wanted their own, personal hedgehog concept. Where *their* passions, *their* best chance of excelling, and what would provide for *their* livelihood could all come together. A business book became a self-help book—a manual to self-discovery.

Why?

Because it danced around the edges of what really is the ultimate journey. Let's not dance—let's net it out. Think about those same three circles in light of what we've been exploring in this chapter.

You have your spiritual gifts and abilities, you have your heart (passion) and experiences, and you have your personality. Where they all come together is everything—that's what you should do. You do what you are. Think of it this way: your spiritual gifts and abilities tell you what to do; your heart and experiences steer you to where you might want to do it; and your personality traits tell you how. Let's say you have the spiritual gift of teaching. You should teach—it's your gift so it's *what* you should do. But if you have a heart for children and positive experiences in working with them, you might want to consider using that teaching gift teaching children. If you are also an extrovert, you should consider having that teaching role with children be used in a way that has lots of engagement and interaction with those children and their parents and even other educators.

Do you see how it works?

Your SHAPE tells you what, where, and how. That's what the Bible is after when it gives us these words from the book of Romans: "Since we find ourselves fashioned into all these excellently formed and marvelously functioning parts in Christ's body, let's just go ahead and be what we were made to be" (12:5 MSG). Are you doing this? Are you letting your SHAPE determine what you invest in and keep you away from what you shouldn't be investing in? Are you letting this guide your life?

Develop Yourself

One last quick word. It's a mistake to think that a spiritual gift is something you are able to *instantly* do *extraordinarily* well without practice and experience. Remember—a spiritual gift is not an instant ability, but a God-given capacity to *develop* an ability. Let's stick with our example of teaching: just because you have the spiritual gift of teaching doesn't mean that you are automatically a good communicator. Your gift may be teaching, but if you have no experience or training in teaching, you will likely be an average teacher in the beginning—even with the spiritual gift of teaching! There may be signs that God has enabled you in that area, but remember—what you have is a supernatural capacity to *develop* the supernatural ability to teach. This is why in a letter to a man he was mentoring by the name of Timothy, the apostle Paul said, "Do not neglect your gift. . . . Be diligent in these matters; give yourself wholly to them, so that everyone may see your progress" (1 Tim. 4:14–15). If you're a Christian, God has given you a spiritual gift, but you have to develop it.

Get in the Game

As we discussed earlier, getting into the game is a benefit of serving. So after you discover your place and begin developing your gifts and abilities, you must get in the game! The goal is to serve in light of all that you are, *with* all you are, in the context of the ministry of the church and for the cause of Christ. This is also how you best fulfill the second step, for the best development is in the course of actual practice. So don't let "time for development" keep you on the sidelines. The Bible says, "*Offer yourselves* as a living sacrifice to God, dedicated to his service" (Rom. 12:1 GNT, emphasis mine). Later that same chapter, it says, "So we are to use our different gifts" (v. 6 GNT). In Colossians we read, "Be sure to carry out the ministry the Lord gave you" (4:17 NLT). And in 1 Peter the Bible says, "God has given each of you a gift from his great variety of spiritual gifts. Use them well to serve one another" (4:10 NLT).

Do you see a theme there?

To discover your gift and get in touch with who you are is key, but it isn't enough. The goal is to put yourself into play! And when you do that, you will reach a level of spiritual fulfillment, energy, and passion that you can't experience any other way. Holistic spiritual vitality and fulfillment can only come when you use your God-given, supernaturally empowered gift in ministry.

Now, let me anticipate what you might be thinking. This all sounds great—in fact, you can get excited thinking about discovering your gifts, finding out where God might want you to invest yourself, and experiencing the thrill of making a difference. You have little doubt serving others would serve your spiritual life well. But you're wondering how you're going to find the *time* to add one more thing to your already crowded, overflowing life. I understand. Let me share a couple of time-related truths that might be helpful and, in ways we all need (myself included), challenging.

First, in our world today, we seem to have an almost compulsive need to automatically fill our schedules. I can take someone's calendar and remove every small group meeting, every ministry involvement, every weekend service, liberating those hours from a person's life. But you know what? In six weeks, they'll just have them filled with something else. It's as if we can't stand a gap in our schedules.

This leads to a second truth. We tend to fill our time with things that don't really matter, creating a life too full for what *is* important. Most of us make to-do lists, but I once heard a speaker comment that what we really need are "stop doing" lists. We tend to be time spenders, not time investors. We can spend our lives engaged in a number of activities; however, when we are at the end of our years, we'll look back and see that our lives didn't add up to very much. Maybe you were busy, you were active, but yours wasn't a life of significance. If you invest your life, however, you have given your life to something you believe in, something bigger than yourself. Many people are heavily spent, and they're very, very busy. They're stretched to the limit. But they are not investing in anything.[10] There comes a time when you say to yourself, *What do I want my life to be like? What am I going to prioritize?* The problem for many of us isn't a lack of time, but how we're choosing to *spend* our time.

Famed psychiatrist Scott Peck once told an interesting story. There was a young Christian woman who lacked any semblance of joy in her life. She suffered from acute depression and was failing to respond to any form of therapy or treatment. Ready to give up on her, Peck was surprised one day to find her bouncing into his office full of joy and excitement. Asking her what was making her feel so good, she said that she was unable to get her car started that morning, so she called a minister friend and asked him if he could drive her to her appointment. He said he would, but on the way he had to stop by the hospital and make a few calls. She went with him, and while he was in the hospital, she visited some elderly people in one of the wards. She read from the Bible and prayed with them. By the time the morning was over, she had never felt better. The emotional uplift was unmistakable. She hadn't felt that good in years.

Instantly, Peck recognized that this woman was benefiting from the investment of serving in an area of giftedness and passion. Peck then pointed out the good news, that they had found the way to make her happy and keep her out of depression. Then, much to his surprise, the woman responded, "You don't expect me to do this sort of thing every day, do you?"[11]

Developing your spiritual life through the practice of servant-hood does not start with your needs, but the needs of others. It does not begin with your schedule, but with what your schedule must *be* in *order* to serve. We are all busy, and we all have competing time demands. The question is whether we will order our lives around what it will take to pursue the Christ life or marginalize the pursuit of the Christ life.

What Could Have Been

Mark Twain once told a powerful story of a man who died and met Saint Peter at the gates of heaven. Knowing that Peter was very wise, he asked a question that he had wondered about his whole life.

He said, "I have been interested in military history for many years. Read everything I could, studied it, went to battlefields and walked the grounds.

"Who was the greatest general of all time?"

Peter said, "Oh, that's easy. It's that man right over there."

The man looked over and he knew him!

He said, "You have to be mistaken. I knew that man on earth. He was just a common, everyday man—he managed a store near my house."

And Peter said, "That's right. But he would have been the greatest general of all time, if he had been a general."[12]

What could you be? Who are you meant to be? What would be the saddest thing imaginable is to be at the end of your life and wonder what you could have been. You've been given a SHAPE that is tied to your purpose in life. Know it, chase it, and fulfill your purpose and destiny.

REFLECTION QUESTIONS

1. Think about a time when you had an opportunity to serve someone else. Does thinking about it in terms of your spiritual life cause you to reflect on it differently? If so, how?

2. Have you ever taken a spiritual gifts test before? Are you already using your spiritual gifts to serve in some way?

3. "Your heart was made by God, is stirred by God, and, if you'll let him, can be directed by God." Are you willing to allow him to do that?

4. What are your natural talents and abilities, including those that have been lying dormant for years?

5. Thinking through your past experiences, what special events do you remember that will help you encourage or counsel others?

6. If you didn't already, take a moment now to think of your hedgehog idea. How will you use it to do what you are?

CHAPTER EIGHT

POSITIONING YOUR HEART

Your heart will always be where your treasure is.
—Jesus, Matthew 6:21 CEV

Money matters. That's why nearly 70 percent of all Americans at the start of the 2020s were planning on making a financial resolution.[1] They're wise. Most people would have their lives profoundly impacted if they could experience financial freedom. If they could get out of debt, have more savings, experience what flows into a life when generosity flows out, they would find it would

change the quality of their family life,

enhance their marriage,

relieve untold amounts of anxiety,

lift them out of states of depression, and

enable them to expand their horizons and vision, whether through additional education, investments, starting their own business, or traveling.

Financial freedom has the potential to set off one of the biggest chain reactions imaginable in a person's life. Just think about family life. A recent study found that the single factor that determined whether having a child would make you more happy or less happy was whether having that child would bring financial strain.[2] Another study found that financial arguments early on in a marriage—whether related to financial stress or not agreeing on basic financial principles—are one of the prime indicators of eventual divorce.[3]

Money matters to God too. There are more verses in the Bible about money than there are about heaven and hell combined: verses on achieving true financial freedom; verses about getting out of debt and building up your savings; and verses about inviting God into the process of money management in such a way that you experience his direct involvement and enablement to achieve financial peace.

Where You Are

There are basically four places you can find yourself in relation to money. These four starting points are not particularly original with me—you can find them netted out in various ways in countless places.

In Trouble

The first place you can be is "In Trouble." This is when you are experiencing financial stress; maybe you're even in crisis mode. You can't pay your bills. The amount you owe has transitioned from showing up as thirty days late on your statement to sixty days, and they've gone from writing you about it to calling you about it. Maybe you've lost your phone service, and now the gas or power company is threatening to do the same. You're a month, maybe two, maybe more behind in your rent or mortgage payments. You're wondering if bankruptcy is around the corner—you've even googled it a time or two. Bottom line: you are in trouble. If this is where you are, you're not alone. Annually, one out of every five Americans will be late on at least one credit card payment.[4]

Looking Good

Another place you can find yourself might be termed "Looking Good." You've got a nice home, two or more cars, fashionable clothes, and took a nice vacation or two this year including some weekend getaways. You've got a Fitbit, just added Disney+ to complement your Netflix stream, and sport the latest iPhone. There are no visible signs of anything

> **WHERE YOU ARE IN RELATION TO MONEY**
>
> IN TROUBLE
> LOOKING GOOD
> DOING WELL, BUT . . .
> GOD HONORING

related to trouble. People look at you and would never think that there are any financial problems at all. But notice what we're calling this: *looking* good. Because looks can be deceiving.

The person who is in this category looks good from the outside, but they're only one or two paychecks away from deep trouble. It's like they're out swimming and having a great time, but there's no lifeguard on duty—nothing protecting them from an unplanned riptide of financial change. Think about how you might answer the following: If you become ill and can't work, or if you are laid off, or if your income is reduced, how long can you survive, financially? If you lose all means of financial support tomorrow, how many days or weeks would pass before you run out of money? Most of us wouldn't last at all. Seventy-eight percent of all Americans, regardless of income, are living paycheck to paycheck.[5] We have no margin, spend everything we make, and have little or no reserves. This means that most of us are fine as long as we keep getting paid. But our finances are in such a condition that if anything were to happen to even one or two paychecks, we'd be over in the trouble category so fast it'd make our head spin. So while many of us may be *looking* good, it's really mostly looks.

Doing Well, But . . .

A third place is "Doing Well, But . . ." You manage your money well, you're not in trouble with debt, and you've got some savings built up in case of emergency, job loss, or health crisis. You're sitting on the beach, nice and easy, having your drink, soaking in the sun and enjoying the waves. But—and this is crucial—your entire orientation is horizontal. Everything in your life related to money is self-oriented. There is no vertical dimension. God isn't even in the picture. So you are doing well financially, but you are not doing well spiritually. You are not honoring God or even thinking about honoring God when it comes to money.

That doesn't mean you're dishonest or lack integrity. It doesn't mean you don't believe in God. It's just that when you sit down to manage your financial affairs it's not a spiritual moment. God's values, principles, and mission aren't on the agenda. It's all about you and what money does for you. It's like you're a functional atheist when it comes to money. It's been said that when someone becomes a Christ follower, the last area of their life that gets converted is their wallet.

The tragic thing is that if you're in this category, it means not only are you excluding God, but by necessity God is excluding you. He's not a part of your financial affairs. He's not being allowed to be on your side. It's all you and you alone. The good, the bad, and the ugly. You're not investing in God, and as a result, he's being kept from investing in you the way he would like.

God Honoring

This brings us to the fourth place you can be. We'll just call it "God Honoring." This is when you are not only doing well financially, but you are doing it in a way that also honors God, recognizes God, and seeks to *please* God. You have both a horizontal *and* a vertical dimension to finances. You follow God's principles in such a way that you avoid crisis, you do more than just look good, and you also do more than simply what it takes to be financially sound and secure. Unlike many people, your money is spiritually aligned with who you are and who you want to be. What you say, what you believe, and what you do are one.

Wherever you are in relation to money, let's look at how you can get where you want to be.

Four Principles

There are four foundational biblical principles for interacting with money. While they are taught throughout the Bible in numerous places, we can find all four principles packaged in a single story Jesus told:

> It's . . . like a man going off on an extended trip. He called his servants together and delegated responsibilities. To one he gave five thousand dollars, to another two thousand, to a third one thousand, depending on their abilities. Then he left. Right off, the first servant went to work and doubled his master's investment. The second did the same. But the man with the single thousand dug a hole and carefully buried his master's money.
>
> After a long absence, the master of those three servants came back and settled up with them. The one given five thousand dollars showed him how he had doubled his investment. His master commended him: "Good work! You did your job well. From now on be my partner."
>
> The servant with the two thousand showed how he also had doubled his master's investment. His master commended him: "Good work! You did your job well. From now on be my partner."
>
> The servant given one thousand said, "Master, I know you have high standards and hate careless ways, that you demand the best and make no allowances for error. I was afraid I might disappoint you, so I found a good hiding place and secured your money. Here it is, safe and sound down to the last cent."
>
> The master was furious. "That's a terrible way to live. . . . If you knew I was after the best, why did you do less than the least? The least you could have done would have been to invest the sum with the bankers, where at least I would have gotten a little interest." (Matt. 25:14–27 MSG)

God Owns It All

The first principle is that God owns it all. Most people who believe in God wouldn't have a problem with that, not if they stop and think about it. If there is a God, then everything we have has been given to us. Our health, our intelligence, our abilities, it all comes from God—everything we have is a direct result of God's enablement. As the Bible reminds us, "You may say to yourself, 'My power and the strength of my hands have produced this wealth for me.' But remember the LORD your God, for it is he who gives you the ability to produce wealth" (Deut. 8:17–18). But it runs even deeper. It's not just that everything comes from God, but that everything *belongs* to God. He's the owner. He made everything to begin with, so it's really his! Here's a quick windshield tour of this principle that runs throughout the pages of the Bible:

> The earth is the LORD's, and everything in it. (Ps. 24:1)

> The land is mine. (Lev. 25:23)

> "The silver is mine, and the gold is mine," declares the LORD. (Hag. 2:8)

> For every animal of the forest is mine,
>   and the cattle on a thousand hills. (Ps. 50:10)

On and on it goes. Of course, the difficulty comes when you begin to pull out some of the implications of God's ownership. For example, if God owns it all then, as the owner, he has all of the rights to what he owns. Since we only have what has been given to us, what we've been allowed to have, then we operate primarily in the realm of responsibilities. This is very much a trust relationship.

Another implication is this: If God owns it all, then every spending decision is a spiritual decision. Whether it's buying a car, taking a vacation, paying taxes, or buying groceries, every spending decision is a spiritual decision, because we are managing the resources

God has given us to manage. He cannot be shut out of any transaction. He cannot be excluded from any purchase, any decision, any investment. We should not be asking, "God, what do you want me to do with *my* money?" Rather, we should ask, "God, what do you want me to do with *your* money?"

The Amount Is Not Important

This brings us to the second biblical principle for money management: The amount is not important. God is not concerned with the amount we are managing, but the management process itself. If you think back on the story Jesus told, the same positive word was said to the person who turned $5,000 into $10,000 as the one who turned $2,000 into $4,000. The question wasn't the amount—the question was faithfulness.

We Are Accountable to God for Our Use of His Money

This leads us to the third major biblical principle for money management: We are accountable to God for our use of his money. If it's his, and we are the managers of what he's allowed us to have, then ultimately we are accountable to him for our management. In the story Jesus told, there was a time when the people with the responsibility stood before the person with the rights, and an accounting of their management was made.

Money Is a Life Test

And finally we come to the last biblical principle related to money: Money is a life test. The only person who was found lacking in

> **FOUR FOUNDATIONAL MONEY PRINCIPLES**
>
> 1. GOD OWNS IT ALL.
> 2. THE AMOUNT IS NOT IMPORTANT.
> 3. WE ARE ACCOUNTABLE TO GOD FOR OUR USE OF HIS MONEY.
> 4. MONEY IS A LIFE TEST.

the story Jesus told was the one who knew what should be done and didn't do it. He had been given a life test, and he failed it. When it comes to our time, our talents, our money, and our resources, we have all been given a little bit for a very short amount of time. It's not ours—everything we have is a gift from God in order to see how we manage it. If we manage it well, we'll be entrusted with more—not just in this life, but in the life to come. The problem is that too often we view money not as a life test, but as life itself.

The Plan

So how do you pass the life test? And not just pass the test, but experience the financial freedom God wants for you? And in real-life ways—freedom from debt, the safety net of savings, the blessings of generosity, and the contentment of having needs met? This happens by following an overarching plan that honors the four principles. It's called the 10–10–80 plan, and it takes the Bible's teaching on financial freedom and organizes it in the simplest way possible: You take whatever you make and manage it by putting 10 percent in one area, 10 percent in another, and 80 percent in a third. If you manage your money this way, you both honor God (and gain all that honoring God brings), and you achieve financial freedom (and all that financial freedom brings).

The First 10

You start off by taking the first 10 percent of everything you earn and giving it to God and his work through the local church of which you are a part. You do that because he has asked you to and because he's the owner, which means he has the right to ask you to do that. In Proverbs 3:9 the Bible says, "Honor the Lord by giving him the first part of all your income, and he will fill your barns with wheat and barley and overflow your wine vats with the finest wines" (TLB). That "first part" is called a *tithe*, meaning

"10 percent," and is the start of the plan. With every paycheck you receive, every dollar you get, give 10 percent to God's work through the local church of which you are a part. You give with trust in one simple fact: no matter how much the amount is, no matter how much it stretches your faith, you will never be able to out-give God.

But don't do it for what you'll get; do it because you know and love God. Do it because you want to pass the life test; do it because your relationship with God matters to you. When it comes to giving, the Bible isn't into guilt trips or manipulation. The apostle Paul went out of his way to make this clear: "Each of you should give as you have decided in your heart to give. You should not be sad when you give, and you should not give because you feel forced to give. God loves the person who gives happily" (2 Cor. 9:7 NCV). You do it as an act of worship.

The Second 10

The second part of the 10–10–80 plan is to take another 10 percent and invest it in some type of long-term savings. With every paycheck, pay yourself. In this area, the Bible doesn't specify a percentage like it does for giving, but most financial counselors recommend the 10 percent figure. This can be investing in mutual funds, stocks, bonds, limited partnerships, pension funds, an IRA, or real estate. This is different than saving for a new piece of furniture or your dream trip to Hawaii. This is about a long-term plan to get money working for you. When it comes to such savings, the Bible has much to say. Here's a sample from the great wisdom book of Proverbs alone:

> Go to the ant, you sluggard;
>   consider its ways and be wise!
> It has no commander,
>   no overseer or ruler,
> yet it stores its provisions in summer
>   and gathers its food at harvest. (6:6–8)

He who gathers crops in summer is a prudent son,
>   but he who sleeps during harvest is a disgraceful son.
>   (10:5)

The wise man saves for the future, but the foolish man
>   spends whatever he gets. (21:20 TLB)

The Bible encourages us to save, and the reason is because of the future. It's not just about wealth building, affluence, or materialistic gain. It's about security and providing for our needs. Without savings, you end up living hand to mouth with little or nothing in reserve.

The 80

So what's the 80 percent for in the 10–10–80 plan? That's what you live on! You give 10 percent back to God, 10 percent into some type of long-term savings or investment plan, and then you use the final 80 percent for your actual living expenses. Here's a spending chart of what it might look like in action:

The 10–10–80 Plan in Action

Total income	$75,000
Less tithe	$7,500
Less savings	$7,500
Less taxes	$15,000
Less debt repayment	$7,500
Balance	$37,500

That's the 10–10–80 plan in action. Give first, save second, live on the rest. But most of us don't live that way. Our spending chart looks a little bit . . . different. As in, the complete opposite. We start off by listing how we want to live in terms of lifestyle: the house we want, the clothes we want to wear, how often we want to eat out, the number of flat screens in place. Then we calculate the debt it takes to fund that lifestyle. Then we pay taxes (again, because we have to), then we try to save a little, and it's usually *very* little. And giving? Forget about it. Even on good days, we tip instead of tithe.

But God's plan, and true financial freedom, doesn't begin with lifestyle. It begins with commitments and priorities. Beginning with the lifestyle you want just puts you into a cycle of debt, shuts God out of the picture, and leaves you without any hope for breaking free. So the 10–10–80 plan calls for a radical rethinking of how you approach money.

I know, you're thinking, *The plan is okay—putting it into place is the kicker. Giving 10 percent, saving 10 percent . . . I can't live off of the 100 percent now! I'm in debt up to my eyeballs and there's no way I can do this. I don't have the ability to even think about this plan.*

> **EXAMPLE OF A TYPICAL SPENDING PLAN**
>
> | | |
> |---|---|
> | TOTAL INCOME: | $75,000 |
> | START WITH LIFESTYLE: | $37,500 |
> | LESS NECESSARY DEBT: | $21,500 |
> | LESS TAXES: | $15,000 |
> | LESS SOME SAVINGS: | $1,000 |
> | GIVING? | $0 |

Let's see if I can help with that, beginning with savings.

Finding the Money to Save

There are two reasons most people don't save money. The first is because they think they don't need to, or they never think about the future in a responsible fashion. The second is because they don't think they can. The first really is foolish; the second is just plain wrong. Let's get wise and deal with finding the money.

A great place to start is to find $10 a day, five days a week, and begin saving it. And finding $10 a day isn't as difficult as you might think. Financial advisor David Bach calls it the "latte factor."[6] The big idea is that we really do have the money to save, but we just waste it—and usually on small things that don't even register to our thinking. Studies show that the number one thing we're doing instead of saving is eating out.[7] Another study found that the average millennial spends more every year on coffee alone than they do toward retirement.[8] Bach developed the "latte factor" after a seminar where a couple came to him after hearing his recommendation to save $10 a day, and they said that they didn't have the money to do it. They said that things were so tight, they couldn't even find $10 a day. So he asked them about their life.

"Let's start in the morning. Before you go to work, do you drink coffee?"

The husband said, "Well, yes."

Bach said, "Great. Where do you get it? Do you make it at home, or do you get it at work for free?"

He said, "Well, neither. We get our coffee on the way to work. We go to Starbucks."

Bach said, "So what do you get at Starbucks?"

And he said that both he and his wife got grande nonfat lattes.

When Bach asked how much these cost, the wife said, "About $3.50 each, so together about $7."

Then Bach said, "And do you get anything to eat with these lattes?"

"Well, yeah, we usually get a bagel or a muffin, and that costs around $3 each, so $6," she said.

"Okay, let's add this up. Seven bucks for two lattes. Six for the muffins. So we're at $13 between the two of you, and you haven't even gotten to work yet." Then he went through the rest of their day and kept finding dollar after dollar being spent in ways they really weren't paying attention to. For them, it ended up being almost $80 a day between lunches out, coffees, and bottled water.

Know that this isn't about dropping Starbucks. The "latte factor" is a metaphor. It's this idea that people can't find even $10 a day to save, yet they're spending a lot more than that on things they don't have to. You can make your own coffee and eat breakfast at home; you can bring your lunch to work instead of eating out; you can take public transportation to work instead of driving. You might drop HBO, or get it cheaper with an online package, or get off cable and use a streaming stick. Maybe you just start to turn off lights when you leave a room. You use coupons at the grocery store. You turn the thermostat up one degree in the summer and down a degree in the winter. You make coffee once a week instead of buying it every single day. You refill a water bottle instead of buying one every time you want some. More money may be available to you than you think.

Miracle of Compound Interest

Let's say you realize how much you are spending on things that you really don't have to have, and you find that $10 a day, five days a week. What would that do?

More than you could possibly imagine.

This is one of the most important financial insights you can ever wrap your thinking around, one that financial money managers know only too well. It's a biblical idea captured in Proverbs 13:11: "Whoever gathers money little by little makes it grow." That is one of the great secrets to wealth building: take a little bit of money and start it growing. And if you invest it in a pre-tax account? Financial management experts call this the miracle of compound interest.

Let me show you what it's about.

If you save just $10 a day, five days a week—which is $2,600 a year—and put that into a pre-tax retirement account that earns 10

▶ **MONTHLY INVESTMENT**

$10 A DAY, FIVE DAYS A WEEK

INTEREST: 10%

1 YEAR =	$2,680
2 YEARS =	$5,460
5 YEARS =	$25,340
10 YEARS =	$72,488
15 YEARS =	$147,511
30 YEARS =	$776,325
40 YEARS =	$2,093,914

percent annually, you'd have almost $5,500 put away in two years. In five years, you'd have more than $25,000. In ten years, more than $70,000. In fifteen years, you'd have almost $150,000. In thirty years, more than $700,000. And in forty years—which is possible if you start at twenty-seven and work until, say, sixty-seven—you'd have more than $2,000,000. All it takes is $50 a week. The secret of compounding interest is time. Over time, money compounds; over a lot of time, money compounds a lot! This is why waiting to begin saving undermines what it can do for your life. Here's another chart to consider.

Monthly	Age	By Age 65 at 10% Return
$300	25	$1,913,334
$300	35	$684,097
$300	45	$230,009
$300	55	$62,265

If you put in $300 a month, starting in your midtwenties, at 10% interest, by the time you're sixty-five, you'll have almost $2 million. But if you wait until you're thirty-five—just ten years—that drops to $684,000. If you wait until you're forty-five, you'll only have $230,000. If you wait to start until you're fifty-five, you'll only save a little more than $60,000. That's the difference time makes.

Debt

At the time of this writing, the total amount of consumer debt in the United States is about $14 trillion.[9] The population of the United States is about 327 million.[10] That means that if you take that debt and average it out to every man, woman, child, and baby, it would come out to $42,813.45 per person.

Or think about credit cards. More than 189 million Americans have credit cards. The average credit card holder has at least four cards in their possession. On average, each household with a

TOTAL AMOUNT OF US CONSUMER DEBT		$14 TRILLION
CURRENT US POPULATION		327 MILLION
AVERAGE AMOUNT OF DEBT PER PERSON		$42,813.45

credit card carries $6,849 in revolving credit card debt.[11] And this doesn't even begin to factor in debt from mortgages, auto loans, or student loans.

What does the Bible have to say about debt? Here's a taste:

The rich rule over the poor,
    and the borrower is servant to the lender. (Prov. 22:7)

Don't run up debts. (Rom. 13:8 MSG)

But don't begin until you count the cost. For who would begin construction of a building without first calculating the cost to see if there is enough money to finish it? (Luke 14:28 NLT)

Does this mean that all debt, no matter what it is for, is bad? No. Debt in general is frowned upon by the Bible, but it doesn't prohibit it in each and every circumstance. In normal economic times you can make a strong case, both financially and biblically, that accepting debt toward an appreciable asset like land, a house, or a building; or a well-thought-through business loan that provides you with some working capital to start a business; or a loan to fund an education that leads to a career is not only appropriate but, at times, even strategic. But that's not the kind of debt most people are enslaved by. What most people are drowning in is consumer debt, lifestyle debt—debt for convenience and pleasure, luxury and appearance.

Debt promises to free us up to get what we want—instant gratification without a downside. But it's an absolute lie. All it does is enslave us to a life of bondage. You might be feeling it right now. Debt is eating up every available dollar you have that could go toward savings or giving, that could go toward a down payment on a house or for retirement. Maybe debt is impacting your marriage, causing stress and friction there. Maybe it's lowering your self-esteem. You have become the servant to the lender, the slave to the creditor, the one in bondage to the debt you carry.

Just think about credit card debt. Let's say you have only one credit card and your balance is just $3,000. You're not behind on your payments. You make at least the minimum payment every month, on time, regular as clockwork. So no problem, right?

Balance	$3,000
Interest	14%
Minimum payment	2%
Time	24 years, 2 months
Total payment	$6,754.78

To pay off a credit card with a $3,000 balance, at an average credit card interest payment of about 14 percent—the national average right now if you have exceptional credit and got a great deal on a card[12]—making the minimum payment (usually about 2 percent of the total amount), would take twenty-four years and two months. Now, at the end of that time (assuming you're still alive) you will have paid a total of $6,754 on that card. That's $3,754.78 in interest, plus the $3,000 principal.

This is a tame example though, because the average amount people carry on their credit card is more than double that, and most people don't have that low of an interest rate. Here's something more realistic:

Balance	$8,000
Interest	18%
Minimum payment	2%
Time	53 years, 9 months
Total payment	$30,931.12

If you carry an $8,000 balance with an 18 percent rate and 2 percent minimum payments, it would take you nearly fifty-four years to pay off. With interest, you would have paid more than $30,000. In other words, your interest would be nearly three times what you actually spent.

Getting Out of Debt

How do we get out of this debt that's holding so many in bondage? It involves four steps. First, make a decision.

There are a lot of people who don't like their life and wouldn't mind things being different than the way they are. But that's a whole lot different than making the decision—down to the core of your being—that there will be change. Change begins with an act of the will, a decision that things are going to be different. There has to be a point in your life where you look at where you want to be, at what you want your life to be like, and then purpose it in your heart to make a change.

> **FOUR STEPS TO GETTING OUT OF DEBT**
>
> 1. MAKE A DECISION.
> 2. SWEAR OFF ALL FUTURE DEBT.
> 3. SET UP A SNOWBALL PLAN.
> 4. CREATE A NEW SPENDING PLAN.

Second, swear off all future debt. You can't get out of debt until you stop getting into debt. You've dug a hole—now don't dig it deeper. Just say no to any more consumer debt that will only leave you more enslaved.

Third, set up a payment plan that begins to reduce your debt. There's a great one for this, and it's called the Snowball Plan. It's the easiest, quickest way to get out of debt. Here's how it works: Take all of your debts—from the MasterCards to the Visas, the mortgage payments to auto loans, college loans to furniture and appliance loans—and then rank them from the smallest balance to the largest.

Once you make your list, start off with your smallest balance and tackle it first. Work on paying it off. Don't worry about the others—just keep making minimum payments on those. Get aggressive with your smallest balance and put everything you can toward it until it's gone. If you get a little raise this year, increase your payment from the minimum of 2 percent to 4 percent, or even higher. If you get a tax refund, use that toward this balance. If you get a windfall of any kind, put that toward it.

Then, when it's gone—and it will go away pretty fast because it's your smallest balance and you're putting all of your effort toward it—take what you were paying toward *that* and apply it toward the *next* smallest balance. Now you have the combined payment amounts going toward your second smallest balance. Make that your focus.

This is why it's called the Snowball Plan: what you pay toward each debt keeps getting bigger and bigger as you eliminate previous debts and add the previous payment amounts from earlier bills to the new payment. By the time you get to something large like a student loan or an auto loan, you're putting a *lot* of money toward it. It will be slow at first, but then it will build with unbelievable speed toward getting out of debt.

So what's the fourth step? Create a new plan! One that will provide a framework for all your future spending decisions, like the 10–10–80 plan. A plan that doesn't start with lifestyle but starts with priorities and commitments. A plan that has honoring God, savings, and being debt-free built into it.

Two Important Questions

Managing money is all about two very important questions. The first is simply, Where is your heart? Jesus talked a lot about money, and always in a way that cut to the chase. Here's how he posed the question:

> Don't store up treasures here on earth, where moths eat them and rust destroys them, and where thieves break in and steal. Store your treasures in heaven, where moths and rust cannot destroy, and thieves do not break in and steal. Wherever your treasure is, there the desires of your heart will also be. (Matt. 6:19–21 NLT)

This is a profound spiritual reality. Where you invest what you have is where you have placed your heart. Where you place your heart will determine how you invest. If your primary investment is in this life, in things, in money for its own sake—if that's what you value most—it will impact your decisions. This will, in turn, impact your heart. That's where your allegiance and your priorities will be. Jesus is asking us to wrestle with a deep and penetrating question: "Where have you taken your heart and, more importantly, where do you *want* your heart to be?" If you want your heart to be with God, then your treasure will be with God. You'll follow his guidelines, his principles, his instructions.

> ▶ **TWO DECISIVE QUESTIONS**
>
> 1. WHERE IS YOUR HEART?
> 2. WHO IS YOUR LEADER?

This brings us to the second question: Who is your leader? Here's how Jesus put it: "No one can serve two masters. For you will hate one and love the other; you will be devoted to one and despise the other. You cannot serve God and be enslaved to money" (Matt. 6:24 NLT). Jesus brings up one of the most fundamental truths of human existence: there is only one true leader in your life. There is only one true God operating in your world. You can no more follow two leaders, or have two gods, than you can walk in two directions at once.

Here's the way it works for a lot of people. They love the Bible's principles on getting out of debt, on saving for the future, and on increasing margins. But they resist giving a full-throated life response to "Where is your heart?" and "Who is your leader?" In other words, they resist the first part of the 10–10–80 plan.

The Tithe

Look at the words of the prophet Malachi that record a kind of dialogue between God and the people.

> "Ever since the time of your ancestors you have turned away from my decrees and have not kept them. Return to me, and I will return to you," says the LORD Almighty.
>
> "But you ask, 'How are we to return?'"
>
> "Will a mere mortal rob God? Yet you rob me.
>
> "But you ask, 'How are we robbing you?'"
>
> "In tithes and offerings. You are under a curse—your whole nation—because you are robbing me. Bring the whole tithe into the storehouse, that there may be food in my house. Test me in this," says the LORD Almighty, "and see if I will not throw open the floodgates of heaven and pour out so much blessing that there will not be room enough to store it. I will prevent pests from devouring your crops, and the vines in your fields will not drop their fruit before it is ripe," says the LORD Almighty. (Mal. 3:7–11)

Now if some of that language was lost on you, here's a quick definition of five key words: *tithe, offering, storehouse, curse,* and *blessing.* As we already defined, the word *tithe* literally means 10 percent, and it was a term that was used for the practice of taking 10 percent of everything you earn—whether through labor or inheritance, windfall or sale—and giving it to God. And it was to be from your firstfruits—meaning the first thing you did with your money, not the last thing you did with what was left over. It was based on all your income. That's the idea behind bringing the "whole tithe."

An *offering* was anything you gave above and beyond your tithe. Ten percent was considered to be the bare minimum anyone would dream of returning to God, since that's the minimum that he had specifically asked for. It was the floor, but never the ceiling. So periodically, out of gratitude and commitment to God, people would give an offering, above and beyond their 10 percent. And the way you would give your tithes and offerings was to give to the storehouse.

The *storehouse* was attached to the temple and was the place where the temple funds, resources, and valuables were stored for use. The temple was the designated place of the people for worship, the center of their community of faith, and the central organizer for ministry for the people of God. Over time, the temple became the local church. In writing to the church at Corinth, this is what the apostle Paul said: "Don't you know that you yourselves are God's temple? . . . God's temple is sacred, and you together are that temple" (1 Cor. 3:16–17).

This is why, throughout the New Testament, the tithes of God's people were to go to the local church of which they were a part. You could give above and beyond offerings to other places, but not the tithe. So the tithe isn't what you give to the United Way or a parachurch ministry or disaster relief—but to your church. And when Jesus was asked his plan, he gave a direct reply: "You should tithe, yes" (Matt. 23:23 NLT). When people don't do this, or they keep everything God gives them, or they don't allocate it the way God asks, it's very serious. It removes them from God's blessing. In fact, not only does it remove them from God's blessing, it actually places them under a curse.

To be under a *curse* wasn't like being under some kind of spell or enchantment like you read about in a fairy tale. In the Bible, to be under a curse from God meant to be outside of his blessing—outside of his umbrella of protection and provision. It meant that you were operating independent of his supernatural oversight and intervention.

So what kind of *blessing* are we talking about here? There are two extremes people can take on what the Bible teaches. The first extreme is to fall into a "health and wealth" expectation that says, "Tithe, and you too can drive a Mercedes because God will get you one." That somehow tithing is the key to seven-figure incomes and ten-thousand-square-foot homes. That is a gross misreading of the Bible. But there's another extreme that's just as off-base. It's the idea that God doesn't bless at all. That there's no relationship at all between what you do financially and what God does.

That's not biblical either.

The Bible teaches—without qualification—that if you follow God in this aspect of financial management, he will bless your life. So again, what kind of blessing are we talking about? Well, it's up to God. It could be financial. It could be a blessing of security, joy, depth of character, fulfillment, impact, influence, or creativity. There can be blessing from God on relationships, marriages, and families. There can be favor shown on an enterprise, an expansion, a breakthrough, or the attempt of a discovery. There is one thing, though, that we can say for sure, because God is very specific about one dimension of how he'll bless us. In the passage from Malachi there was a reference to God protecting crops from pests and fruit from spoiling—God is making it clear that those who follow him in this area will never have to worry about their giving taking away from their supply. We can rest assured that we will not lose ground because of our generosity. If we give 10 percent, God will make the 90 percent go just as far, if not farther. He will supernaturally care for our needs.

It's as if God is saying, "Listen, trust me enough and care about me enough to do what I say in this area of financial money management. In return, I will become supernaturally involved in your life in a unique way, bringing incredible levels of blessing—including a specific blessing that you will never have to worry that your giving will leave you without enough for your own needs. Take care of your money in the normal ways—don't binge, don't go crazy with debt. Do your part, and I'll do mine."

Practical Steps

But how do you move toward the 10–10–80 plan when you can't live off the 100 percent you're making now, much less 90 percent? In fact, the whole 10–10–80 plan, while it sounds great, seems almost like a fantasy.

That's why we've been walking through how to make this happen. It's why with savings, we talked about the latte factor and finding the money to save. It's why with debt, we talked about using the Snowball Plan to focus on your smallest bill, and then when that's gone, applying that focus to the next and then the next.

And it's why with giving, the goal is to work toward a tithe.

It's not all or nothing. You can start gradually and work your way up. This is an important biblical idea. Over and over in Scripture, you see God calling his people to do something, and it's often a huge task. His first word is usually not "Accomplish this," as much as "Begin this." For example, when God led the Israelites to the promised land, he told them that they would have to take possession of it. And it was a lot of land to possess! It could take months—maybe years! But notice the language God used when he put this to them: "Begin to take possession of it" (Deut. 2:24).

He didn't say, "I expect you to accomplish this at once" as much as he said, "I expect you to *start* this at once, and I'll be with you every step of the way." It's the same with our money. It's as if God is saying, "Start toward this. Get moving. I'm not expecting you to be able to pull this off overnight. You've been managing your financial life outside my principles—we both know that. So this is a seismic shift. It's going to take some time. But start. Position your heart. Acknowledge me as leader. Honor me. Trust me. *Begin*."

You may not start with 10–10–80; it's going to be more like 1–1–98. That's legal! In fact, it's not only legal, for most people it's a necessity. So begin to work toward a full tithe, giving even 2 or 3 percent, but with a commitment to keep increasing it as you move toward greater levels of financial freedom. God will be delighted with that, and he'll be delighted with you.

Why? Because he knows what's going on in your heart, and he knows that you've positioned him as leader.

With each step, you can take this promise from Jesus to heart: "So don't worry at all about having enough food and clothing. . . . Your heavenly Father already knows perfectly well that you need them, and he will give them to you if you give him first place in your life and live as he wants you to" (Matt. 6:31–33 TLB).

REFLECTION QUESTIONS

1. Why does our relationship with money reveal our heart and character?

2. What is God's foundational financial principle? What difference should that principle make in how we deal with money?

3. What does God get from tithing? What do I get by honoring God in this way?

4. What examples can you give of times in your life when you have seen God outgiving you?

5. What steps are you going to start taking today to work toward the 10–10–80 plan in your life?

CHAPTER NINE

ACHIEVING MAXIMUM IMPACT

> *I [am] an atheist. . . .*
>
> *I don't respect people who don't proselytize. . . . If you believe that there's a heaven and hell and that people could be going to hell . . . how much do you have to hate somebody to not proselytize?* —Penn Jillette[1]

What is the most important, strategic, life-changing thing you could ever do for another human being? That is, if you really wanted to make a difference? If you *really* wanted to impact their life? You could become an educator and teach those who are illiterate how to read. You could go to medical school and become a doctor and heal the sick. You could enter politics and work to pass laws that protect the vulnerable or serve the poor or bring justice to the oppressed. You could start a soup kitchen and feed those who are hungry or malnourished. You could join the military and defend freedom wherever it is threatened around the globe.

All of these would make a difference, wouldn't they? And all are important. We need people investing their lives in every single one of those ways, and more. But they are not the greatest thing you can do for another human being. They are not what makes the maximum impact on another life. What makes the maximum impact on a human life is when you are involved in bringing about the intersection of their life with the living God through Christ in such a way that their entire eternity is altered. When you do that—when you introduce someone to Jesus and invite them to give their life to him—you are making the biggest possible impact on another human being imaginable.

Let's pause right there.

I know I may have just lost you. While as a Christian you most certainly do believe Jesus matters, that there is an eternity facing all of us, and that someone's relationship with Jesus is everything to where and how you spend that eternity, the whole idea of talking about your faith to someone else is beyond awkward for you to even think about. It's the last thing you would ever want to do with anyone. Someone bringing Christianity up, or you bringing it up with *them*, is your worst relational nightmare. The thought of sharing your faith causes you to hyperventilate, the hives break out, a panic attack sets in, and you need a pair of adult Depends.

Or maybe there's a different impediment for you. Yes, you believe it all, but it's just not that real to you or something you viscerally feel. If you're honest, you don't look at other people with spiritual empathy in terms of where they are or how they are doing and what kind of eternity they're facing. You meet all of this with a spiritual yawn. This is why the average person who considers themselves a Christ follower never talks about their faith with other people. Even worse, half of all millennial Christians think it's *wrong* to evangelize another person.[2]

Oh my.

I want to make the case that this is what matters *most* in terms of impacting other people. I want to remind you that every life on this planet, no matter what the circumstances of their life might be, would be better if they had Christ at the center of it. Every life would be better if they could experience real liberation from guilt and shame that comes through even a single drink from the well of grace Christ offers and, through that, to experience the forgiveness of sin.

Every life would be better with a deep and clear sense of true north in terms of navigating what's right and wrong, true and false, good and bad.

Every life would be better with the pulsating energy of the Holy Spirit coursing through their veins, changing and transforming them from the inside out into someone who is more loving, more joyful, more peaceful, more patient, more kind, more good, more faithful, more gentle, and more self-controlled.

Every life would be better experiencing the new community Christ came to establish, where you can love and be loved, know and be known, serve and be served, celebrate and be celebrated. You've never locked eyes with someone whose life would not be better with Christ. I want you to have that truth dominating your thoughts and emotions as you interact with their lives.

This is why I want you to see how you can share your faith with those you care most about in a natural, authentic, compelling way. I want you to gain a comfort level talking to friends about Jesus, the same way you would feel comfortable talking to them about a movie they ought to see or a series on Netflix they should binge. I want you to experience the absolute rush of seeing someone come to Christ through your efforts, your invitation, your words, your friendship. To see them burst through the waters of baptism, make a beeline to you, and say, "I don't know how to thank you for caring enough about me to tell me about Jesus."

But first, let's take a closer look at why this really is the biggest impact you can make on someone's life.

Heaven and Hell Are Real

First and foremost, it's because heaven and hell are real, and real people go there. I know, we don't like to think about hell. We don't like to talk about hell. But if hell is real, as I quoted Penn Jillette saying in the epigraph, how much would you have to hate someone not to talk to them about it? How much would I have to hate you—believing to the core of my being that heaven and hell are real places and real people go there—to not try to keep you out of it? That would be off-the-charts hate.

Why does evangelism matter? Because heaven and hell are real, and real people go there.

When Jesus talked about hell, he wasn't trying to beat people up with it, or tell everybody they were going to go there because they were bad people. Jesus talked about hell to try to keep people *out* of it. I've always been taken by a story Jesus told when he was trying to ratchet up the intensity among his followers so they would understand how real this is. He told a story about what happened to a man five minutes after he died, after a five-minute taste of hell. Here it is:

> There was a rich man who was dressed in purple and fine linen and lived in luxury every day. At his gate was laid a beggar named Lazarus, covered with sores and longing to eat what fell from the rich man's table. Even the dogs came and licked his sores.
>
> The time came when the beggar died and the angels carried him to Abraham's side. The rich man also died and was buried. In Hades, where he was in torment, he looked up and saw Abraham far away, with Lazarus by his side. So he called to him, "Father Abraham, have pity on me and send Lazarus to dip the tip of his finger in water and cool my tongue, because I am in agony in this fire."
>
> But Abraham replied, ". . . Between us and you a great chasm has been set in place, so that those who want to go from here to you cannot, nor can anyone cross over from there to us."
>
> He answered, "Then I beg you, father, send Lazarus to my family, for I have five brothers. Let him warn them, so that they will not also come to this place of torment." (Luke 16:19–28)

Jesus told that story for some very important reasons. First and foremost, Jesus wanted to drive home the fact that everybody dies.

The rich man was full of life and had what anyone would call a good life. In the story, Jesus tells us that he was clothed in purple and fine linen, code in that day for the highest end of wealth. Death was the farthest thing from the rich man's mind, and nobody would have even thought about bringing the end of his life to his attention. But then he died. Jesus's point? No matter who you are, or what your life is like, death is inevitable.

Jesus also told this story because he wanted to make it absolutely clear that when we die, it's not the end. It's just the beginning of an eternity spent in either heaven or hell. But that's still not all. Jesus also wanted to make it clear that where we go for eternity will be based on the decisions we make *in this life*. There are no second chances after we die. And then finally, did you notice the last thing Jesus brought out in his story? The reality that hell immediately makes anyone a flaming evangelist.

When the rich man realizes his state, his heart is suddenly full of rabid concern for those still alive who he cared about. He never cared about them spiritually before for a single moment of his life. Suddenly he realizes that telling them was everything! Once he knew hell was real, then nothing else mattered more than saving people from it. The need for a rescue was absolutely overwhelming.

This drove Jesus's life and consumed him. He talked about it nonstop, every chance he could. Let me take you to just one moment in his life that shows you how passionate he was about this. It's found in Luke's biography of Jesus: "Now the tax collectors and sinners were all gathering around to hear Jesus. But the Pharisees and the teachers of the law muttered, 'This man welcomes sinners and eats with them'" (Luke 15:1–2).[3]

Now stop there and think about that scene for a minute. Here was Jesus, spending time with people of incredibly ill repute. Tax collectors, who were infamous for swindling people and extortion. And "sinners," meaning people with foul mouths, who had made mistakes, cheated people out of money, slept in all the wrong beds, and made a habit of lying; irreligious people who hadn't darkened the doorstep of a church in ages; people who lived lives that went against everything that the religious leaders of the day stood for. These "sinners" were all gathering around Jesus, listening to him, taking in everything he had to say. They were even eating with him, and he with them. And that's not an insignificant detail.

In the culture of that day, if you ate with someone it was like saying, "This is my friend. This is someone I care about. This is someone I am bringing into the intimacy of my life. This is someone I affirm as having worth and value." This is why the religious leaders of that day wouldn't eat with someone who didn't meet their standards. And why they made a point to remark, "He even eats with them."

It was meant to be cutting.

But the people Jesus ate with were captivated by this man who—while compromising nothing—welcomed them, spent time with them, and talked with them about a God who loved them, cared about them, and wanted to be in relationship with them. And the purpose of that relationship was not to condemn and critique, but to love them and forgive them. Jesus told them about a God who wanted to lavish them with forgiveness, grace, and a new beginning. While this whole interplay was happening, the religious leaders gathered together in their holy huddle and said, "Can you believe this guy? What is he thinking? They're the enemy! Doesn't he know that we've separated ourselves from them? Why, he even acts like he likes them! You'd think that his whole mission was all about . . . them!"

That was the closest they got to the truth. What's interesting is that Jesus apparently heard them muttering. They were . . . I don't know . . . maybe a hundred or so yards away, yet Jesus knew exactly what they were saying (kind of a God thing). The Bible says that Jesus then turned and went to them, and was so upset that they didn't get what the heart of the Father was about—so upset that they didn't see the truth and the spiritual reality of these dear people's lives—that he told not one, not two, but three straight stories to rapid-fire truth into their lives and set them straight. And if you're a Bible trivia nut, this is the only time in all of recorded Scripture where Jesus was so upset that he told three straight stories to make one point.

The three stories he told were of a lost sheep, a lost coin, and a lost son. In the first story, someone charged with a hundred sheep lost one. He was so concerned that he left the ninety-nine and embarked on an all-out search-and-rescue mission to find that one lost sheep. And when he found it, he threw a party.

The second story told of a woman who had lost one of ten coins—a tenth of her entire estate—so she began a painstaking sweep through every inch of her home until she found it. And when she finally did, she threw a party.

Then, in one of the most poignant stories Jesus ever told, a father had lost his son—at least lost him relationally. The son went to his father and asked for his inheritance before his father even died. If you know anything about the culture of that day, this was a heartbreaking slap in the face to their whole relationship. He was telling his father, in essence, that he wished he was dead. Brokenhearted, the father gave the son his inheritance. The son took off, squandered all of his inheritance on wild living, and ended up with nothing. The economy then took a downturn, and the son had to work for next to nothing on an agricultural farm. Things got so bad, and his poverty and hunger so intense, that he decided to go home to his father and ask for forgiveness. You can imagine how low he had to reach to do that. He even prepared a speech and rehearsed it, saying, "Father, I have sinned against heaven and against you. I am no longer worthy to be called your son; just take me back, even as a hired hand."

When he headed down the final road to his home, there, waiting for him, was his father. A father who had been standing on the front porch, looking, longing, hoping. A father who had probably been doing this at sunup before work every day, and then went right back on the porch at sundown after the workday ended.

When the father saw his son, he lost it—he ran down the road to him. Again, in the ancient Near Eastern culture of that day, no father ever did that. It would have been demeaning to the father. The role of the son was to come and grovel. And then maybe the father would show leniency. More than likely he'd be punished.

But in Jesus's story, the father picked up his robe and ran to his son, embraced him, kissed him, and put new clothes on his back, shoes on his feet, and rings on his fingers. Then he threw the most extravagant party imaginable in honor of his wayward son, saying, "For this son of mine was dead and is alive again; he was lost and is found" (Luke 15:24).

Jesus finished those stories and then looked into the eyes of the religious leaders and asked, "Do you not get it? Do you not get what's going on in this world and the spiritual realities of heaven and hell?" In those stories, Jesus made it clear what his mission on this planet was about, and what ours is to be as well. In all three stories, what was lost mattered—and mattered deeply—to the person who lost it. In all three stories, there was nothing that mattered more than finding what was lost.

If you have ever lost something that you love, you search for it. The greater the value of what is lost, the more urgent, the more all-encompassing, the more determined the search is.

If you have ever lost something that you love, you search for it. The greater the value of what is lost, the more urgent, the more all-encompassing, the more determined the search is. Whenever I think of this, I think about how, many years ago, when the church I now lead and also planted was in its early days, we met at an elementary school. Every weekend we had to set up and break down the church.

One weekend we were breaking down after the service, putting things back in trucks and sheds and cars, and my wife, Susan, and I looked around and realized that our daughter, Rebecca, wasn't there. I thought she was with Susan and Susan thought she was with me. She was only about seven years old at the time. At first, we only panicked a little, because we assumed she'd be found right around the corner.

But she wasn't right around the corner.

She wasn't out on the playground, she wasn't in any of the rooms, she wasn't in the hallway, she wasn't in the cafeteria, and she wasn't in the gym. We couldn't find her anywhere. I have seldom experienced such sheer panic and fear. My little girl, gone. Missing.

I started racing through the building, going into rooms we didn't even use, hallways that were darkened. I ran out front and yelled her name until I thought I was going to lose my voice. Nothing mattered more to me than finding my daughter. It occupied every thought, every ounce of energy. Everything else paled in comparison.

Just as we were going back over every inch of the school again, and getting ready to call the police, I saw something. Down a long, dark hallway that we didn't use, outside of the doors we always blocked off because they led directly to the back fields, I saw a little head with brown hair barely above the glass. She had gone out the door and it had locked behind her, so she had sat down where she couldn't be seen and was just waiting for someone to find her. She had been crying and she was scared, and she didn't know what to do but just wait.

I ran down that hallway, threw open those doors, grabbed that little girl, and held her like you would not believe. You could not have pried her from my arms.

That is the heart of God toward his children.

He is completely taken with those who are lost, occupied with the thought of not finding them. The heart of the Father is one in absolute, ongoing search mode. Jesus wanted to make it absolutely clear that there is nothing more critical than seeking what is lost in order for it to be found.

Nothing.

Jesus never let up on this—it coursed through every teaching, every message, every conversation, every action. If you have any doubt, read his words:

> Who needs a doctor: the healthy or the sick? I'm here inviting outsiders, not insiders—an invitation to a changed life, changed inside and out. (Luke 5:31–32 MSG)

> Your Father in heaven . . . doesn't want to lose even one. (Matt. 18:14 MSG)

> [I] came to seek and to save the lost. (Luke 19:10)

If you still have any doubts about the passion of Jesus for seeking the lost, look at the scene of his crucifixion (Luke 23:39–43). What was he doing during those last agonizing moments, with life and blood draining from his body? He was working to try to save one more.

Even then.

Don't tell me this isn't the heart of God. Don't tell me this isn't his passion. Don't tell me this isn't his mission.

Don't tell me this isn't the maximum impact you can make on a human being. Don't tell me that.

And don't tell Jesus that.

The driving force, the ultimate reality, of Jesus's life was that he was sent on a mission. And that mission was singular in focus. It was to those who were far from God. Why? Because he knew something more clearly than anyone else who had ever lived or ever would: that heaven and hell are real, and real people go to one or the other. This is also why at the end of those three stories he told, at the end of every search-and-rescue operation, there was a party. The finding was always marked by celebration.

That's always God's attitude when someone returns. The Bible says that there is rejoicing all across heaven when even a single person turns to Christ—the moment someone becomes a Christ follower, offers their heart to him. The moment the words leave the lips of their heart in prayer asking Christ to be their Leader and Forgiver, at that moment, all of heaven—from one end to the other—all the saints who have died and have gone before, the legions of angels all across heaven, and the Father, Son, and Holy Spirit gather together and throw a raucous party. The banner over the head table has that person's name on it.

Why?

Because the greatest impact possible on that life has been made.

What Evangelism Isn't

Let's say you're in. You agree with the apostle Paul when he wrote,

> Because we understand our fearful responsibility to the Lord, we work hard to persuade others. . . .
>
> And God has given us this task of reconciling people to him. For God was in Christ, reconciling the world to himself, no longer counting people's sins against them. And he gave us this wonderful message of reconciliation. So we are Christ's ambassadors; God is making his appeal through us. We speak for Christ when we plead, "Come back to God!" (2 Cor. 5:11, 18–20 NLT)

How, then, do you answer this question, also posed by Paul? "But how can they call on him to save them unless they believe in him? And how can they believe in him if they have never heard about him? And how can they hear about him unless someone tells them?" (Rom. 10:14 NLT). Obviously the Bible is asking these questions rhetorically. Nobody's life will be impacted for Christ unless somebody impacts it for Christ.

So how do you do that? How does someone who is a Christ follower impact someone spiritually in a positive way who isn't a Christ follower? I can tell you what won't reach those who are far from God. They won't read a tract that you leave in a bathroom stall. They won't listen to Christian radio or podcasts or watch

Christian television or movies. They won't read a bumper sticker that says "Jesus Loves You" and feel like pulling their car over to the side of the road and reorienting the entire trajectory of their life.

So how do you impact a life for Christ? The answer is you become an evangelist. I know this immediately raises images of somebody pushy, obnoxious, loud, opinionated, and annoying—everything you hate. You probably don't even like the word *evangelism* itself. Probably the first thing that enters your mind is going out and knocking on people's doors or standing on a street corner with a bullhorn.

Trust me, I get it.

When I was a sophomore in college, literally just a few weeks after I had become a Christ follower, I was invited to a weekend retreat with some other folks from a Christian campus ministry. So I went. It ended on a Sunday, and before we left we all planned to go to a local church together.

Now I had never really gone to church at that point, but I knew enough to know you were supposed to get dressed up—at least, back in those days. I had brought along this old pair of dress pants from high school, a blazer that I had from graduation, and a Bible someone had given me. I was all dressed up but felt uncomfortable wearing clothes from high school that were a little tight.

I had some time to kill before we left when I saw this drink machine and decided to go get a soda. I put in my money and pushed the button, but when I bent down to get the can . . . yes, my pants ripped. And not just your average, everyday little rip. It would have settled the boxers or briefs question for any inquiring mind.

I just froze there scrolling through options in my mind. There weren't many. So there I was, bent over, when out of nowhere comes this woman from behind me (of course). I remember she said, "Oh, I see you've got a problem."

I said, "You see very well."

She said, "Do you want me to help you get that fixed?"

I said, "Yes, that would be great!"

So we jumped in her car and started down the road. At first I didn't say anything—conversation wasn't exactly on my mind. I just assumed she lived nearby, and we were going to go to her house for a quick repair job. Then I noticed that she was looking up and down every street while she was driving, as if she didn't have a clue as to where she was going.

I thought, *I am in a car with my underwear hanging out, with a stranger who told me she was taking me somewhere, and she doesn't seem to know where!*

So finally I asked her, "Do you know where we are going?"

She said, "No."

And she didn't say anything else, and I didn't know what else to ask. But then, being a master of communication, I said, "So, like, um . . . what are we doing?"

And she said (I kid you not), "I'm looking for someone going out for their Sunday morning newspaper so that we can pull in and ask to use their sewing machine. Don't you think that would be a great way to get to know someone who may not know the Lord?"

I remember thinking, *NO, I DON'T!*

But before I could tell her that wasn't my style of evangelism—though my pants could be a visual for the parting of the Red Sea—she spotted some old lady coming out of her house and whipped into the driveway. In a state of shock, I heard her say, "Excuse me, we were on our way to church and he split his pants. Do you have a sewing machine we could use?"

What killed me was that this lady didn't bat an eye but said, "Sure, come on in!"

Before I knew it, I was handing my pants out through the cracked door of a bathroom, waiting for the repair job in the bathroom with the lady's poodle (but that's another story). Through the cracked door I heard them talking about Jesus while the lady sewed up my pants.

I walked away from that experience mortified—I mean scarred for life. And I remember thinking, *If that's what it means to connect with others about Jesus, I'm out. I mean, I love Jesus and everything, but . . .*

That isn't what this is about.

Invest and Invite

The core dynamic of evangelism is investing and inviting.[4] Let's start off with the invest part. Investing in someone is simply about building a relationship. Getting to know them, spending time with them, entering into community with them. Only within the confines of a relationship will there be the trust to be authentic and to have conversations about what matters most in life. You already have these relationships built into your life. You have friends, family members, neighbors, coworkers. You've got people you interact with through your kids at school or with sports teams.

But if you're going to make an impact on them for the cause of Christ, you've got to be intentional about those relationships. You've got to serve those relationships. You've got to invest in them as someone who is on mission for them and their life. You're going to pray like mad for them. You're going to pray for your time with them. You're going to pray for openings to talk about spiritual things, opportunities to let them get to know you and how Christ has intersected the deepest needs of your life.

The core dynamic of evangelism is investing and inviting.

And those openings will come. The fact that you're a Christ follower will come out. You'll have chances to peel back the layers and tell your story: what you were like before Christ and what life has been like after. The ways you ran from God and chased after anything and everything else, and then what it was like when you finally came home. You can tell them the difference your relationship with Christ has made in your marriage. The difference it's made in the lives of your kids and your parenting.

Then comes the invite part. Along the way, they'll have good, fair, honest, and reasonable questions. They may want to explore, and they may be intrigued by your life. They may see something in your life (and I hope that they do) that they don't have themselves. That's where the invite part comes in. Invite them to come and see, come and hear, come and explore. This tandem of investing and inviting is at the heart of the mission.

It always has been.

Do you know how Jesus not only gathered his first followers, but how the whole Christian movement burst onto the world scene? This is from John's biography of Jesus in the Bible:

> The next day John [the Baptist] was there again with two of his disciples. When he saw Jesus passing by, he said, "Look, the Lamb of God!"
>
> When the two disciples heard him say this, they followed Jesus. Turning around, Jesus saw them following and asked, "What do you want?"
>
> They said, "Rabbi" (which means "Teacher"), "where are you staying?"
>
> "Come," he replied, "and you will see."
>
> So they went and saw where he was staying, and they spent that day with him. It was about four in the afternoon.
>
> Andrew, Simon Peter's brother, was one of the two who heard what John had said and who had followed Jesus. The first thing Andrew did was to find his brother Simon and tell him, "We have found the Messiah" (that is, the Christ). And he brought him to Jesus.
>
> Jesus looked at him and said, "You are Simon son of John. You will be called Cephas" (which, when translated, is Peter).
>
> The next day Jesus decided to leave for Galilee. Finding Philip, he said to him, "Follow me."
>
> Philip, like Andrew and Peter, was from the town of Bethsaida. Philip found Nathanael and told him, "We have found the one

Moses wrote about in the Law, and about whom the prophets also wrote—Jesus of Nazareth, the son of Joseph."

"Nazareth! Can anything good come from there?" Nathanael asked.

"Come and see," said Philip. (John 1:35–46)

John pointed Andrew to Jesus, then Andrew invited Simon Peter, then Philip invited Nathanael, and on and on it went. This was all happening like people talking to someone about a great restaurant, or a new movie, or a great blog or website. Or the way people post about something on Facebook. It was such an organic thing. People were sharing about Jesus like gossip over the backyard fence. Natural, real, authentic, conversational.

I remember being in a conversation with a guy I was just starting to get to know. This was several years ago, but it was so typical of countless conversations I've had with people. We met because our sons were on the same basketball team down at the YMCA. We would just talk here and there, nothing big, but we were hitting it off and obviously liked each other. I had no idea where this guy was spiritually. Well, actually I did have a hint or two because whenever his kid shot a bomb, he dropped a bomb of his own.

Then, just a few weeks into our relationship, he asked me what I did for a living. Part of me thought, *I really wish I could delay that one a few days*, because when people find out I'm a pastor some of them start treating me like I'm a third sex. Other people start going back over in their minds all of the things that they've said that they probably shouldn't have. Some are just shocked.

This guy fell into the shocked category, and he said, "Really? No way! You seem so normal!"

And I said, "Thank you . . . I think."

Then he just started talking about his church background, and he said, "I used to go to church when I was a kid and I hated it. My mom just shoved religion down my throat, and I haven't been in years." He just went on like that, talking about it. There we were having this conversation on the sidelines of our kids' basketball game, it got into spiritual stuff, and you know what?

It was just so normal and so natural. It wasn't that big of a deal at the end of the conversation for me to say, "I don't want to put words in your mouth, but tell me if this is kind of what you're saying. It sounds like you've given up on church, and church people, but not on God. Is that fair?"

And he said, "Yes, that's exactly what it is."

Then I said, "Well . . . now this is going to sound really weird . . . but the church I pastor? It's kind of a church for the unchurched. It's full of people just like you who've given up on church but not on God. And everyone there will pretty much be in your camp, coming from an unchurched background, and with the same kinds of questions you have. I'd love for you to give it a shot sometime. If you're game, I'll meet you out front and walk you around to make sure you're acclimated. And then maybe we can get some lunch afterward. And that's a standing invitation. I'm going to come back and ask you again if I don't see you soon, because I think you're going to love it."

It's so easy to do this. You can do this even when you're not in that close of a relationship with someone. For example, someone at work says, "Hey, how was your weekend?"

You say, "Well, we went out Friday night, saw a movie. Saturday did some lawn work and some soccer games for the kids. We went to church. The music was amazing, and our kids love it. The messages really connect with us. So yeah, good weekend!"

You know what often will happen?

Most of the time they'll say, "I haven't been to church in ages. Where do you go?"

And then you can give them your answer. Nothing forced, nothing big, just an invitation. But a powerful one. The latest study I saw found that 80 percent of our friends—people we know, people we work with, people in our neighborhood, people we're investing in—would come to church if we invited them.

Just ask yourself. Did you come to Christ because of an advertisement on TV or in a newspaper? Did you come to Christ because somebody you didn't know handed you a tract or knocked on your door? Or did you come to Christ because you were invited to a church or evangelistic event by someone you knew—either a friend, relative, or somebody you worked with?

I think I know your answer.

Ken Gire writes of a man by the name of Scott Manley who reached out to high school students on the campus of Arlington Heights High School in the late sixties. "He showed up in a pair of Converse All Stars, gym shorts, T-shirt, a handshake, and a smile. Several of us on the basketball team were playing a pickup game in the gym, and this young seminary student from Southwestern Baptist Theological Seminary worked his way into the game. Over the weeks ahead he kept showing up. At lunch. After school. In the parking lot. And before long, he worked his way into our lives."

Scott was working through a ministry called Young Life that builds relationships with high school students, establishes clubs, and sponsors Bible study groups, all for the purpose of reaching out with the saving message of Christ in places where churches often cannot go. Ken reflects that he doesn't remember any of Scott's talks, only the music of the message: *I love you. I care about you. You matter. Your pain matters. Your struggles matter. Your life is sacred and dear to God. He has a future for you, plans and hopes and dreams for you, and blessings for you.* And the music streamed into Ken's heart, and Ken became a Christian, going on to Texas Christian University, where he turned around and led a Young Life club himself. Also on the leadership team was a young woman named Judy, who would one day become Ken's wife. Judy had become a Christian through a classmate, who had become a Christian through her Young Life leader, who had become a Christian through . . . *Scott Manley.*

One day, Ken and Judy ran into Scott at a conference they were attending together, along with three of their four children. Judy, who had never met Scott, went up to him and said, "You don't know me, but I'm Judy Gire, Ken Gire's wife." They hugged, then she continued. "There's something I've been wanting to tell you for a long time." Years of emotion welled up inside her. "Scott, you were instrumental in leading my husband to Christ. You led my Young Life leader to Christ. My Young Life leader led a friend of mine to Christ. And this friend told me about Christ. You are my spiritual heritage. These are three of our four children. This is Kelly, and she knows Jesus. This is Rachel, and she knows Jesus. This is Stephen, and he knows Jesus. And Gretchen, our oldest, she isn't here, but she knows Jesus too. All of us know Jesus because of Scott Manley. Thank you so much. Thank you."

Scott threw his arms around her, and for a long time they wept together.[5]

Don't let evangelism scare you or put you off. It's one of the most important and rewarding investments you can ever make—not only for your own spirituality, but for the spiritual lives of others in our world. Just ask Ken and Judy. Or ask me. Even better, just ask yourself.

Samuel Shoemaker once wrote a poem that captures the importance of this for us all:

> I stand by the door.
> I neither go too far in, nor stay too far out.
> The door is the most important door in the world—
> It is the door through which men walk when they
>   find God.
> There's no use my going way inside, and staying there,
> When so many are still outside and they, as much as I,
> Crave to know where the door is.
> And all that so many ever find
> Is only the wall where a door ought to be.
> They creep along the wall like blind men,
> With outstretched, groping hands,
> Feeling for a door, knowing there must be a door,

Yet they never find it . . .
So I stand by the door.
The most tremendous thing in the world
Is for men to find that door—the door to God.
The most important thing any man can do
Is to take hold of one of those blind, groping hands,
And to put it on the latch—the latch that only clicks
And opens to the man's own touch.
Men die outside that door, as starving beggars die
On cold nights in cruel cities in the dead of winter—
Die for want of what is within their grasp.
They live, on the other side of it—live because they have not
     found it.
Nothing else matters compared to helping them find it,
And open it, and walk in, and find Him.
So I stand by the door.[6]

And so should we all.

REFLECTION QUESTIONS

1. Who first shared with you about Christ? Who has recently been a great spiritual encouragement to you?

2. Can you think of someone right now who you need to invest in and invite? Maybe more than one someone?

3. If someone were to watch you for a week, how would they know that you are a Christian?

4. What character quality in a Christian would most attract someone else to consider Christ?

CHAPTER TEN

KEEPING IN STEP

Since we live by the Spirit, let us keep in step
with the Spirit.—Galatians 5:25

On Halloween night, 2010, a series debuted on cable that, if you had read the description about it, probably wouldn't have grabbed your attention as being anything beyond typical Halloween fare. Based on a comic book about survivors trying to make it after a zombie apocalypse, it was called *The Walking Dead*. It became the most watched show on cable and, for younger demographics, the most watched show of any format—cable, broadcast, or internet. It's been nominated for Golden Globe awards, Writer's Guild awards, and Emmys. It's called *The Walking Dead* because that's what the zombies are—dead people who are still walking around, devouring anything and everything in sight. But if you've seen it, you know that it's really not about the zombies. It's about the survivors. Their challenges, their struggle to find safety, their constant attempts to stay alive. You also find that what's often worse than the zombies are the other human survivors—many of whom have resorted to the worst cruelties to stay alive.

The Bible doesn't speak about the walking dead, but it does speak of the idea of the *waking* dead. More than two thousand years ago the power of God was reflected in a single life with such a clear demonstration of might and energy that all of human history was forever changed, culminating in raising that life, physically, from the dead. Through the resurrection of Jesus, God demonstrated his ultimate power—because there is no greater power on earth than power over death.

As if that was not amazing enough, the Bible tells us that the very same power that raised Jesus from the dead is available for your life: "[You need to] understand the incredible greatness of God's power for us who believe him. This is the same mighty power that raised Christ from the dead" (Eph. 1:19–20 NLT). The word for "power" used in that verse in the original Greek language was the word *dunamis*, and it is where we get our word *dynamite*. It's the same word used when referring to the power behind Jesus's miracles. And as we just read, it is the power that raised him from the dead.

That's some power.

The Bible says that power can be there for you. Think about that. The power that resurrected Jesus can resurrect your life too! As a Christ follower, you know about the physical aspect of this in that physical death isn't the final word. We look forward to being resurrected from the dead and spending eternity with God. But that's not the only kind of resurrection the Bible talks about, or the only kind of application of resurrection power the Bible puts forward. You can be resurrected from the dead *now*, spiritually, while you are still walking this planet. No matter where you are or where you've been, God can bring you to life from any place you feel lifeless. He can give you whatever new beginning you need. The power that coursed through the veins of Jesus, the power that raised him from the dead, can bring you back to life as well. As the apostle Paul wrote to the church in Rome, "And just as Christ was raised from the dead by the glorious power of the Father, now we also may live new lives" (Rom. 6:4 NLT).

So why isn't this happening in more lives? Why isn't this happening in your life? It's because we aren't keeping in step with the Holy Spirit, the one who works in us to bring us back from the dead.

The Holy Spirit

What comes to your mind when I say the word *ghost* or *spirit*? Is it something like the cartoon character Casper the Friendly Ghost? Is it Slimer, the little green guy who "slimes" people in *Ghostbusters*? Are you a hopeless romantic, and when you hear the word *ghost*, you can only think of Patrick Swayze?

Now, what comes to mind when I say, "Holy Ghost"?

As we bring our journey through the dynamics and investments of spiritual growth to an end, I've saved what is arguably the most important for last. This chapter is about the Holy Spirit, someone many Christians know very little about. Let's make sure that doesn't include you.

When it comes to the Holy Spirit, the Bible gives us a handful of fundamental truths that we need to get down. The first truth about the Holy Spirit is that the Holy Spirit is *God* the Holy Spirit, the third person of the Trinity. The Bible teaches that the nature of God is triune—that God is three persons who are one God. There is God the Father, God the Son, and God the Holy Spirit. Not three Gods, but one God, who is composed of three persons. That's what *Trinity* means—three in one. While each person has a unique role and ministry, each also shares all the attributes of God.

So just like God the Father and God the Son, God the Holy Spirit is eternal. Genesis tells us he was active in creation. Like God the Father and God the Son, he is omnipresent, meaning present everywhere and at all times. As Psalm 139:7 says, "Where can I go from your Spirit?" The answer is nowhere, because he is

> **THREE TRUTHS ABOUT THE HOLY SPIRIT**
>
> 1. THE HOLY SPIRIT IS GOD.
> 2. THE HOLY SPIRIT IS PERSONAL.
> 3. THE HOLY SPIRIT IS IN YOU.

everywhere. In Acts 5, we are told that to lie to the Holy Spirit is to lie to God. Why? Because of the fundamental truth that the Holy Spirit is God.

The second basic truth about the Holy Spirit is that he's personal. Throughout the Bible, the Holy Spirit is referred to as a person. Most people think of the Holy Spirit as a force or an "it," but he's a "he." The difficulty stems from our mental perception. We can wrap our heads around the idea of Father and Son, because visual images probably pop into our minds. Perhaps we think of an actor like Morgan Freeman, who played the role of God in *Bruce Almighty*, or Jim Caviezel, who was the actor cast as Jesus in *The Passion of the Christ*. But the Holy Spirit? He's harder to make a movie about. It doesn't help that many people were raised with the King James Version of the Bible running through their heads that referred to him as the Holy Ghost. But "Holy Ghost" is not the best translation of the original Greek. It's most accurate to call him the Holy Spirit.

Yet while Spirit, he is still deeply personal. Jesus always referred to the Holy Spirit in personal terms, not as an "it" but as a "he"—a *person*. Not only is the Holy Spirit referred to in personal terms throughout the Bible, particularly the New Testament, but throughout the Scriptures the Holy Spirit is attributed all the components of personality—a mind, feelings, and a will. We read that he thinks, grieves, makes decisions. . . . He is fully personal.

But here's what is most important to understand about the Holy Spirit in regard to your spiritual life: the Bible teaches that the Holy Spirit is in you. When you cross the line of faith—when you come to Christ as Forgiver and Leader—the Holy Spirit enters your life. He takes up residence; he moves in and sets up house. Inviting Christ into your life is essentially inviting the presence and work of the Holy Spirit.

Jesus talked about this a lot, particularly toward the end of his ministry here on earth. He wanted to help his followers understand what transition would take place when his time on earth was over.

John's biography of Jesus records Jesus saying, "But very truly I tell you, it is for your good that I am going away. Unless I go away, the Advocate [the Holy Spirit] will not come to you; but if I go, I will send him to you" (John 16:7). In essence, Jesus was saying, "When I leave, I'm not abandoning you. I'm going to send the Holy Spirit. And his work, his ministry, his presence is so decisive that it's actually good that I'll be gone! It will be better to have him in you than me with you!"

Why did Jesus feel that way? Because through the Holy Spirit, we have God entering into our heart and changing us from within. That's why one of the main words the Bible uses for the Holy Spirit is Counselor from the Greek word *paraclete*, meaning "one who walks alongside." So the Holy Spirit is with us always, and he has one big item on his agenda: to make us more and more like Jesus. To help shape us, mold us, and form us into someone who looks and talks and thinks and lives more like Jesus every day. Romans 8 says, "You are not controlled by your sinful nature. You are controlled by the Spirit if you have the Spirit of God living in you. (And remember that those who do not have the Spirit of Christ living in them do not belong to him at all)" (v. 9 NLT).

This is a critical idea, because it's the heart of our hope and the power for life change. We are changed through the work of the Holy Spirit in us. The Holy Spirit inside of us is the power of God unleashed in our life to make us more like Jesus. His work in our life is to form Christ in us. Only the Holy Spirit can penetrate into the hidden recesses of our personality and transform us from the inside out in ways that are supernatural. In and through the Holy Spirit there is power to control the evil and cultivate the good within us. In and through the Holy Spirit there is power to take whatever is dead and bring it to life. Or, if need be, to put to death whatever is killing us.

You may wonder, "So if I'm a Christian, and I already have the Holy Spirit, then why do I have areas where I know I'm lifeless?" Because of one simple truth that's true for all of us: If you're a

Christian, while you have the Holy Spirit *in* your life, the deeper question is how much the Holy Spirit has *of* your life. Yes, you already have all the Holy Spirit you will ever have. But how much does the Holy Spirit have you? Whatever areas of your life he does not have will be like unanimated tissue. Lifeless. Not like Jesus at all. This is why the Bible talks about the importance of being filled with the Holy Spirit.

Be Filled

Coming to Christ is not the same as staying in Christ, much less growing in Christ. We've already learned that once you become a Christian, the Holy Spirit takes up residence in your life. But then the Bible gives this very direct challenge: "[Now that you have the Holy Spirit] . . . be filled with the Spirit" (Eph. 5:18). Paul was writing this to the church in Ephesus to a group of people who were Christ followers. They already had the Holy Spirit, and Paul was then telling them "now be filled."[1]

I once tried to illustrate this dynamic during a sermon with two large jars, both filled with water to the same level. By the side of one jar I had a large box of Alka-Seltzer tablets, wrapped in their foil packets. By the other, the same size box, but with each of the tablets already unwrapped. I told those attending the service to think of each jar of water as representing a person's life, and both of them were Christians. But one hasn't unleashed or unwrapped the Holy Spirit. At this point, I threw the wrapped tablets into one of the jars. Obviously, nothing happened. My point was that this represented a Christian who hadn't allowed the Holy Spirit to penetrate, to spread out, or to fill their life.

Then into the other jar I threw the unwrapped tablets. They immediately filled the water in the jar with bubbles of energy. As we watched, I mentioned how when we unwrap and unleash the power and presence of the Holy Spirit, he will fill every nook and cranny and will impact every area of life. The point? Just as both jars had

Alka-Seltzer inside them, all Christians have the Holy Spirit; but you can have the Holy Spirit in your life without his filling.

This was a tame demonstration, to be sure. When it comes to unleashing the power and presence of the Holy Spirit, we're talking about the power that raised Jesus from the dead. We're talking about the third person of the Trinity, God the Holy Spirit, working in your life. So then, I moved to something with a bit more voltage. I took a two-liter bottle of Diet Coke with a Mentos "geyser tool" on top of it that drops six Mentos in, creating a twenty-five-foot eruption. You may have seen this experiment done on YouTube.

Let's just say it made the point a bit better.

"Be Being Filled"

So how do you unleash the presence and power of the Holy Spirit in your life? Let's go back to Paul's letter to the church in Ephesus that read "be filled with the Spirit" (Eph. 5:18). The original Greek phrase "be filled" is grammatically a present imperative—we don't have a smooth English translation for this except "be filled." To really get at the idea of the original Greek, you would need to read this verse as "be being filled" or "keep on being filled." Further, it's in the passive voice, meaning it's not "fill yourself up with the Spirit," but "let yourself be filled" or "let the Holy Spirit fill you."

The Bible teaches that an individual is filled with the Holy Spirit by involving himself or herself in the process that leads to an ongoing, day-in, day-out filling. It's not a once-for-all experience, but an ongoing process. It's a way of doing life. Whenever we talk of something being filled, we usually have an image of something like a glass being filled with water. Whenever the Bible talks about being filled with the Holy Spirit, that's not what it means. We are not vessels into which God pours a certain amount of Holy Spirit. The Holy Spirit is a person, so being filled is a relational issue.

So how do we experience "being filled with the Spirit"? Well, it's not about levitating or foaming at the mouth. To be filled with the Holy Spirit means that we allow him to occupy, guide, and control ever-increasing areas of our life. It's a simple idea, but a profound one. The more you follow the Holy Spirit, the more you are filled. And the more you are filled, the more you are led. And the more you follow that lead, the more you are filled again. The entire dynamic is that you live in and by and through the Spirit, being led by the Spirit, keeping in step with the Spirit, surrendering daily to his leadership and promptings.

So much of this book has been about the kinds of things needed to unwrap the Holy Spirit in your life—to keep on being filled. To live a life that follows the inner workings and promptings and voice of the Holy Spirit. Just think about reading and reflecting on the Bible in the context of a quiet time. Guess who wrote the Bible? The Holy Spirit! Guess who speaks to us through the Bible? The Holy Spirit!

When we listen to the words of the Bible and the inner promptings of our own spirit as it is nudged and guided by the Holy Spirit, we are being led to become that which we naturally aren't—increasingly like Christ. We are led to make choices; to say yes to things or no to things; to do this, but not do that. To feel certain ways, think certain ways, act certain ways.

How does this work in day-in, day-out life?

I was taking an international flight out of the airport and it was delayed late into the night. People were irritable and tired, and I was especially frustrated because I was going to be missing a connecting flight that I had to make that was going to throw my whole itinerary into disarray. Then it was announced that the flight was overbooked and they had to try to bring in another plane, and everyone began jockeying for position to try to get a seat on the first plane.

My own mood and spirit were no different than anyone else's. Maybe worse. It didn't help that, as I was trying to maneuver my way through the group to ensure I had a seat on the first plane, there was this one guy who was just in my space. He was bumping against me, trying to get ahead and elbow his way to get in front of me. Feeling Jesusy, I was bumping him right back, holding my ground and place in the makeshift line. He glared at me, and I glared right back.

In truth, there was nowhere for any of us to go.

Then he said, "Look, you keep bumping into me."

I said, "Well I don't have anywhere to move! People are bumping me!"

Then I glared again, almost daring him to say anything else. It was a very pastoral moment.

We both eventually made it on the plane, with the guy I had been jostling with just two seats back from where I was seated. After I took my seat, I felt the Holy Spirit just sweep over my conscience, as if saying, "Well Jim, that was mature. I raised you better than this! You were rude and aggressive with that man and reflected nothing of Jesus to him or to anyone else."

I was so convicted, and at that moment I was also reminded of something I had been reading earlier that day in Scripture: "Love is patient, love is kind and gentle, not quick to anger . . ." (1 Cor. 13). So there I was with the Holy Spirit and with Scripture, and it was so clear to me the prompting that I had: "Get up, walk back two seats, and apologize to that guy. Get up out of your seat while there is still time, and you go back to him and you apologize."

I thought, *But I don't want to!*

Yet I knew what Scripture said, I knew I had just acted like a jerk, and I had this deep, unmistakable Holy Spirit–generated conviction running through me telling me to get up and go.

Hit the Pause button with me for a minute: This truly was a pivotal moment where a lot more was on the line than you might think. I had already taken a step back spiritually over the last forty-five minutes, and here was a chance to reclaim ground that I had already lost. In terms of being filled with the Holy Spirit, at that moment, I was leaking pretty bad. And that's what "be being filled" is about—moment by moment, choice by choice, prompting by prompting.

Okay, hit Play. I got up, walked back the two seats, and suddenly loomed over the man unexpectedly. He flinched. It's embarrassing to say this, but he probably thought I was coming to do anything but apologize. I leaned over to him and said, "You know it's been a long day and we're all tired, and I really acted like a jerk back there. I'm sorry and I need to ask for your forgiveness."

Then I held out my hand for a shake.

He was obviously stunned. But he shook my hand and said, "No worries."

Now this is not a "me being a hero story," it's a "me being a jerk story." It feels like there are a thousand times when I don't follow the Spirit's promptings. But the point is that when I do, I am keeping in step with the Spirit. It's like we're this big block of granite, and the more that we allow the Holy Spirit as Sculptor to work, chipping away at us, the more the image of Jesus begins to materialize through the stone.

But the work of the Holy Spirit is not just direction and guidance, promptings and convictions. The Holy Spirit provides the raw power, the raw experience of God that we need to follow through. Our effort toward coming to life, becoming more and more like Jesus, is not just a human effort. Had it not been for the power of the Holy Spirit in me, I would never have gotten out of my seat and walked back those two rows of seats. So it's not just human effort. It is our effort combining with the power and presence of the Holy Spirit in our lives. That's how you unleash the Holy Spirit in your life.

And again, it's deeply relational.

This is why the Bible talks about grieving the Holy Spirit through our sin. Think about it this way: he's trying to make you more like Jesus. He's leading, guiding, and prompting you toward that end. When you give in to patterns of sin, or when you leave sin unconfessed and unaddressed in your life, then you are turning the Holy Spirit away, shutting him out, refusing his work.

You are rejecting him.

This grieves him relationally and diminishes his power and presence in your life. That in turn allows you to return to states of deadness, or to stay dead and never experience the life that could come. We all do this. Yet none of us *have* to. As the apostle Paul wrote to the church at Ephesus:

> Since you have heard about Jesus and have learned the truth that comes from him, throw off your old sinful nature and your former way of life, which is corrupted by lust and deception. Instead, let the Spirit renew your thoughts and attitudes. Put on your new nature, created to be like God—truly righteous and holy.
>
> So stop telling lies. Let us tell our neighbors the truth, for we are all parts of the same body. And "don't sin by letting anger control you." Don't let the sun go down while you are still angry, for anger gives a foothold to the devil.
>
> If you are a thief, quit stealing. Instead, use your hands for good hard work, and then give generously to others in need. Don't use foul or abusive language. Let everything you say be good and helpful, so that your words will be an encouragement to those who hear them.
>
> And do not bring sorrow to God's Holy Spirit by the way you live. . . .
>
> Get rid of all bitterness, rage, anger, harsh words, and slander, as well as all types of evil behavior.
>
> Instead, be kind to each other, tenderhearted, forgiving one another, just as God through Christ has forgiven you. (Eph. 4:21–32 NLT)

We all have pockets of our life that reflect the walking dead. Through the Holy Spirit, we can wake whatever is dead in us. So let's return to our question: As a follower of Jesus you already have as much of the Holy Spirit as you are ever going to have,

. . . but how much of *you* does the Holy Spirit have?

Life in the Spirit

For Robertson McQuilkin, president of Columbia International University, it became quite a life test. It was during a vacation in Florida when Robertson saw the first sign.[2] His wife, Muriel, repeated a story she had just told five minutes earlier to some friends they were visiting. Then it began to happen more and more frequently. Three years later, when she was in the hospital for testing, a young doctor pulled Robertson aside and told him that he may need to consider the possibility that his wife had Alzheimer's.

He didn't believe it. He didn't want to believe it.

Then her memory deteriorated even further. They went to a neurologist, and after a battery of tests, it was confirmed that she did indeed have the disease. Her loss of memory turned into an inability to even continue a train of thought. Soon she could neither read nor write. She never knew what was happening to her. Where once there was a vibrant, creative, articulate person, there was now a process like a slow death, a light dimming out, a fade from life itself.

McQuilkin found himself torn between two commitments, two divine callings: the growing needs of his wife, and the demands of his career. He made the decision to approach his board of trustees with the need to begin the search for a successor, so that when the day came when Muriel needed him full-time, she would have him. He was fifty-seven years old at the time, and it seemed unlikely she would hold out until he could retire naturally at sixty-five.

They didn't want to act on his request. They made no plans. While he appreciated their response, he knew it was neither realistic nor responsible. This led to years of struggle over what should be sacrificed—his role as president or his role as caretaker to his wife. His trusted, lifelong friends urged him to stay at the helm. They told him that institutionalizing his wife was the best course, and that his wife would grow accustomed to her new environment.

All he could think of was whether anyone would love her in such a place, let alone love her as he did. He had often seen the empty, listless faces of those lined up in wheelchairs along the corridors of bare hallways, waiting for the fleeting visit of a loved one.

For a while he arranged for a companion to stay with her in their home so that he could go into the office each day. By this time, she had lost much of her comprehension and could hardly express any of her thoughts. Yet when he would leave, she would take off after him trying to follow wherever he went. Sometimes she would follow him out as many as ten times a day. At night, when he helped her undress, he would find her with bloody feet.

When he told the doctor, the doctor's eyes filled with tears. All the doctor could choke out was, "Such love she has for you." Then he explained that the characteristics developed across the years come out at times like these. Her heart's longing was always to be with him, to be near him, and now this was how all of those feelings were being channeled.

But being with her was not easy.

When they went to the grocery store, she would begin to load other people's carts and take off with them. She would refuse to eat or take a bath. He was used to meeting multimillion-dollar budgets and designing programs to grasp emerging global opportunities, but none of that was as demanding as this. The tension built—full-time with Columbia, or full-time with his wife—and his wife's deteriorating condition made the moment of decision draw ever near.

Again, his friends circled around him and told him that he was at the peak of his impact and influence as president, while he could not really do anything else for his wife. Then the time finally came. He had to decide. And decide he did. The Holy Spirit made the prompting clear.

Robertson McQuilkin resigned as president of Columbia.

This is what he said to the students and the board of trustees:

I haven't in my life experienced easy decision making on major decisions, but one of the simplest and clearest decisions I've had to make is this one, because circumstances dictated it. Muriel now, in the last couple of months, seems to be almost happy when with me, and almost never happy when not with me. In fact, she seems to feel trapped, becomes very fearful, sometimes almost terror, and when she can't get to me there can be anger . . . she's in distress. But when I'm with her she's happy and contented, and so I must be with her at all times. . . . And you see, it's not only that I promised in sickness and in health, till death do us part, and I'm a man of my word. But as I have said (I don't know with this group, but I've said publicly) it's the only fair thing. She sacrificed for me for forty years, to make my life possible, . . . so if I cared for her for forty years, I'd still be in debt. However, there's much more. . . . It's not that I *have* to. It's that I *get* to. I love her very dearly, and you can tell it's not easy to talk about. She's a delight. And it's a great honor to care for such a wonderful person.[3]

What was the title of the book he wrote in the midst of caring for her, shortly before her death?
Life in the Spirit.

REFLECTION QUESTIONS

1. What comes to your mind when you hear "Holy Spirit"?

2. What comes to mind, in relation to your own life, that might be keeping the tablets—the power of the Holy Spirit—wrapped up and sealed in your life?

3. When was the last time you felt a clear prompting from the Holy Spirit? Did you obey it?

4. What do you know, right now, you are doing in your life that is grieving the Holy Spirit?

AFTERWORD

The Committed Life

When Christ calls a man, he bids him come and die. —*Dietrich Bonhoeffer*[1]

In his newspaper column called "Market Report," Bill Barnhart once talked about the difference between investors and traders in the stock market. He said that a trader makes decisions on a minute-by-minute basis, wheeling and dealing, pursuing short-term profits. Traders may have no confidence whatsoever in the companies in which they buy stock. All they're after is an immediate payoff. An investor, on the other hand, buys stock based on their views of the company. Investors are in it for the long haul. They chain themselves to the mast. They commit their money to a stock, believing that over time, the stock will pay dividends and grow in value. The ups and downs of the market don't scare them, because they believe in the quality of the company, its leaders, and its product.[2]

When it comes to your spiritual life in Christ, you have to decide whether you are going to be an investor or a trader. Which one you choose will determine *everything*. Following Jesus is not an idea, much less a philosophy. It's a tangible, life-changing *act*. It's something that you *do*. It's a fundamental, settled choice within your very being—a choice that not everyone who desires a spiritual life is willing to make.

There was a provocative series of three encounters worth noting, captured by Luke, between Jesus and some who said they wanted to be his followers. Here is the first:

> As they were walking along the road, a man said to [Jesus], "I will follow you wherever you go."
> Jesus replied, "Foxes have dens and birds have nests, but the Son of Man has no place to lay his head." (Luke 9:57–58)

This person seemed to be willing to follow Jesus. He was quick to say, "Count me in! Wherever, whenever, however." You'd think that Jesus would be thrilled that someone would have that kind of attitude. But did you notice how Jesus responded? In essence, he said, "I don't think you get it." To really choose to follow Jesus means to know what it is you're choosing, and then to commit to the choice. Jesus knew that commitment was not to be taken lightly; once he even said, "Whoever wants to be my disciple must deny themselves and take up their cross daily and follow me" (Luke 9:23). For Jesus, that language wasn't just demonstrating a flair for the dramatic. It was literal. Jesus knew that his cross was real—an instrument of ancient, cruel torture that resulted in humiliation; raw, excruciating pain; blood; ripped flesh; and eventual death.

Following Jesus isn't about sitting at the feet of some guru for a seminar at a retreat. It isn't about having a nice, comfortable, safe dose of spirituality in your life to make you feel good whenever your thoughts run deep about ultimate questions and eternal destinies. Jesus called people to *follow* him, and there was only one place he was going—*a cross.*

The true nature of spiritual living involves sacrifice, duty, and commitment.

Then there was this second person Jesus encountered:

> He said to another man, "Follow me."
> But he replied, "Lord, first let me go and bury my father."

> Jesus said to him, "Let the dead bury their own dead, but you go and proclaim the kingdom of God." (Luke 9:59–60)

This person wanted a life with Christ but wanted to put off what it would take, or at least put the investment on hold. When this man said that he wanted to go back to bury his father, that didn't mean he simply wanted to go back and attend his dad's funeral. It was a Hebrew phrase that meant he wanted to go back and *wait* for his father to die, to be available in case there was anything he needed to do whenever his father *did* die. His father may not have even been sick! He was saying that his life, with its issues and concerns and responsibilities, was more important than following Jesus.

So when it came to the call to follow Christ, he essentially said, "Not now, Jesus, it's kind of a bad time for me. My life's really full, and I've got a lot on my plate. But I really want to *give* to you, I really do want to put you first. But right now, it's just not a good time." This is so common it feels like I've heard a thousand variants. A man will say to me, "Yeah, I'm going to work really hard now, so that I can retire early, and then I'm going to give my life to ministry." Or they'll say, "Yeah, as soon as I pay for this house, get my retirement covered, and get the kids through college, then I'm going to really start giving." It hardly ever happens. It's just an excuse to put off doing what God is calling them to do with their life now.

Jesus never let anybody get away with anything. Did you notice how he replied? *"Let the dead bury the dead."* To paraphrase, "Let those who are spiritually lifeless order their life around things that don't have any eternal significance. You show signs of life—or at least act like you *want* to be alive—so *live* like it! Let those who care more about the material world than the spiritual world build their lives and commitments and decisions around goals and efforts and investments that won't matter at the end of a life. I'm calling you to invest in the kingdom. And that's not an investment for a season, but the investment of a life."

Jesus's reply, in short, was "put up or shut up."

Then came a third encounter:

> Still another said, "I will follow you, Lord; but first let me go back and say goodbye to my family."
>
> Jesus replied, "No one who puts a hand to the plow and looks back is fit for service in the kingdom of God." (Luke 9:61–62)

This man didn't jump in and say yes without thinking about the cost. He didn't put Jesus off and say, "Well, maybe later." This guy had a different twist—he said, "Okay, I'll follow you, *but* . . ." Then he added a condition, he inserted a qualification, about the *degree* to which he would follow Jesus. In his case, the qualification seemed reasonable, didn't it? All he wanted to do was go say goodbye to his family. But that wasn't what was really going on. The issue wasn't saying goodbye. We can see that from how Jesus responded to him. Jesus saw right through his words to what was really going on. It wasn't about saying goodbye to his family, it was about *not* wanting to say goodbye to his previous way of life. He wanted to say yes to Jesus while holding on to what he *had* been following and to the priorities he *used* to pursue. Jesus's reply made it very clear that he had no use for that kind of following.

To follow Jesus means that your heart is *fully his*, not divided in its loyalties. Jesus didn't want little professions and half-hearted commitments or weak, watered-down responses. He didn't want people to think that following him was something tame that could be done on the side in someone's spare time. Following him could never be a matter of "Yes, BUT—let me do this, or not do that, go back here, cling to this, keep doing that," and yet make you feel, the whole time, like you were really following. It's as if Jesus said, "You're wanting just enough spirituality to feel good about yourself, but not enough to change your life. That's not what this is about."

It's worth noting that not a single one of these men wanted to turn Jesus down. Not a single one said, "No, I don't want to follow you." They *wanted* what they knew in their hearts that following Jesus would bring to their life. They wanted to feel good about themselves spiritually and to develop themselves spiritually. They wanted Jesus in their life. What they *didn't* want to do was what it would take, which was *commitment*.

Sometimes I wonder if we have forgotten what commitment really entails. Encountering it seems so alien to our sensibilities. I ran across an old book once that has now become a prized part of my library. It was a biography that was simply titled *Borden of Yale '09*. It told of a man named William Borden who went to Yale University as an undergraduate and afterward became a missionary candidate for China. Heir to the Borden Dairy estate, he was already a millionaire by the time of his high school graduation. As a gift on the event of his graduation from high school, Borden was sent on a trip around the world. As he traveled throughout Asia, the Middle East, and Europe, he experienced a growing concern for the hurting and lost of the world. He wrote home to say, "I'm going to give my life to prepare for the mission field." After making this decision, he wrote two words in the back of his Bible: "No Reserves."

From there he went on to Yale University, but with purpose and determination. During his first semester, he began a movement among the students that spread throughout the campus to gather, read the Bible, and then pray. By the end of his first year, 150 fellow freshmen were meeting for weekly Bible studies. By the time he was a senior, 1,000 of Yale's 1,300 students were joining together in these groups. Beyond the campus, Borden founded the Yale Hope Mission to reach out to those on the streets of New Haven. Yet all was in view of his sense of call to foreign missions, which soon had a focus on Muslims in China. After graduation, he was offered numerous high-paying jobs, all that he declined to pursue the mission field. At this point, he wrote down two more words in the back of his Bible: "No Retreats."

Borden next went to graduate school at Princeton Seminary, where he was ordained to the ministry. After he finished his studies, he set sail for China through the China Inland Mission, stopping first in Egypt to study Arabic. While there, he contracted cerebrospinal meningitis. In less than a month, William Borden was dead. He was twenty-six years old. But before his death, knowing that the steps of his life would take him no further, he wrote two more words in his Bible: beneath "No Reserves" and "No Retreats" he wrote "No Regrets."[3]

I don't want you to lead an "almost" life. A life that could follow Jesus fully but chooses against full commitment. A life that chooses the things of the world over the things of God. And that is what is key—realizing the stark nature of the choice. The apostle Paul had a breakthrough on this in his life:

> But whatever were gains to me I now consider loss for the sake of Christ. What is more, I consider everything a loss because of the surpassing worth of knowing Christ Jesus my Lord, for whose sake I have lost all things. I consider them garbage, that I may gain Christ and be found in him. (Phil. 3:7–9)

According to Paul, knowing Jesus, having Jesus, being in relationship with Jesus, made everything else pale in comparison. In fact, all those other things he now viewed as only garbage. Even the word he used for *garbage* revealed the depth of his resolve. It was a very earthy term. The word Paul used was *skuvala*, and it was the term for manure or dung. And not just any word for manure or dung. *Skuvala* was the slang for manure or dung. In other words, back in Paul's day there would have been bumper stickers that said things like, "Skuvala happens." That was how Paul evaluated choosing the world over Jesus, choosing this life over the life to come. The "almost" life as compared to full devotion.

So here's my final challenge. Don't take your one and only life and *almost* live for Jesus.

Completely live your one and only life for Jesus.

SUGGESTED READING

I highly recommend the following books for the ongoing development and growth of your life in and with Christ. This is not meant to be an exhaustive list on all things related to faith. These are books for the ongoing growth and maturation of your relationship with God, intentionally limited to twenty-five titles. If someone in my church asked me for a short list of titles to help them grow in their walk with Christ, barring perhaps a few titles of my own, this is the list I would give them.

Thomas à Kempis, *The Imitation of Christ*
Dietrich Bonhoeffer, *The Cost of Discipleship*
Charles Colson, *Loving God*
Brent Curtis and John Eldredge, *The Sacred Romance*
Elisabeth Elliot, *Through Gates of Splendor*
Gordon Fee and Douglas Stuart, *How to Read the Bible for All Its Worth*
Richard Foster, *The Celebration of Discipline*
Ken Gire, *The Reflective Life*
Phillip Keller, *A Shepherd Looks at Psalm 23*
Thomas R. Kelly, *A Testament of Devotion*
Brother Lawrence, *The Practice of the Presence of God*
C. S. Lewis, *Mere Christianity*
Gordon MacDonald, *Ordering Your Private World*

Brennan Manning, *The Ragamuffin Gospel*
John Ortberg, *The Life You've Always Wanted*
J. I. Packer, *Knowing God*
Eugene Peterson, *A Long Obedience in the Same Direction*
Suzanne Stabile, *The Road Back to You*
John R. W. Stott, *Basic Christianity*
Charles Swindoll, *Improving Your Serve*
Corrie ten Boom, *The Hiding Place*
Rick Warren, *The Purpose Driven Life*
John White, *The Fight*
Dallas Willard, *The Spirit of the Disciplines*
Philip Yancey, *What's So Amazing about Grace?*

NOTES

Chapter 1 Identities, Deceptions, and Myths

1. Henri J. M. Nouwen, *Life of the Beloved: Spiritual Living in a Secular World* (New York: Crossroad, 1993), 26.

2. W. David O. Taylor, "Seminary Grads: God's Name for You Matters More Than Your Masters," *Christianity Today*, July 16, 2019, https://www.christianity today.com/pastors/2019/july-web-exclusives/seminary-grads-gods-name-for-you -matters-more-than-masters.html.

3. On this, see Joachim Jeremias, *The Prayers of Jesus* (Philadelphia: Fortress Press, 1967), 96. Talmudic reference: *b.Ber.* 40a (Bar.) par *b. Sanh.* 70b (bar.).

4. For example, see the chapter on "Unchristians" in James Emery White, *Christianity for People Who Aren't Christians* (Grand Rapids: Baker, 2019).

5. Philip Yancey, *The Jesus I Never Knew* (Grand Rapids: Zondervan, 1995), 132.

6. Philip Yancey, *What's So Amazing About Grace?* (Grand Rapids: Zondervan, 1997), 198. See also, *The Babylonian Talmud, Book 1: Tract Sabbath*, trans. by Michael L. Rodkinson (1903), chapter XXIII, http://www.sacred-texts.com/jud/t01 /t0135.htm#fr_179.

7. Thomas Kelly, *A Testament of Devotion* (New York: Harper and Row, 1941), 19.

8. Adapted from Chuck Swindoll, *Living Above the Level of Mediocrity* (Waco: Word, 1987), 58.

9. Yakov Smirnoff Quotes, Goodreads, accessed January 20, 2020, https:// www.goodreads.com/author/quotes/754003.Yakov_Smirnoff.

10. C. S. Lewis, *The Screwtape Letters* (New York: MacMillan, 1982), 11.

11. Richard Foster, *The Celebration of Discipline* (San Francisco: Harper and Row, 1978), 1.

12. This analogy is a contemporized version of one given by Dallas Willard in *The Spirit of the Disciplines: Understanding How God Changes Lives* (San Francisco: Harper and Row, 1988), 3–4.

13. Dallas Willard, *The Divine Conspiracy* (New York: HarperSanFrancisco, 1998), 273.

14. On this, see Willard, *The Divine Conspiracy*.

15. Megan Fowler, "In Christ, Alone: Most Believers Say They Don't Need Others for Discipleship," *Christianity Today*, August 22, 2019, https://www

.christianitytoday.com/news/2019/august/lifeway-discipleship-assessment-growth-alone.html.

16. I am indebted to C. S. Lewis, particularly *The Screwtape Letters*, for this insight.

17. Ken Gire, *The Reflective Life* (Colorado Springs: Chariot Victor, 1998), 47.

Chapter 2 How to Bible

1. Martin Luther, *Table Talk*, ed. and trans. by Theodore C. Tappert, in Luther's *Works*, vol. 54 (Saint Louis: Concordia Publishing House/Fortress Press, 1967), H57.

2. "63 Fascinating Google Search Statistics," Bluelist.co, accessed January 2020, https://bluelist.co/blog/google-stats-and-facts/.

3. The following section adapted from White, *Christianity for People Who Aren't Christians*, 135–48, as these aspects of reading the Bible are critical to both believers and explorers.

4. On this, see William W. Klein, Craig L. Blomberg, and Robert L. Hubbard Jr., *Introduction to Biblical Interpretation*, 3rd ed. (Grand Rapids: Zondervan, 2017).

5. Gire, *The Reflective Life*, 90.

6. Adapted from Gordon MacDonald, *The Life God Blesses* (Nashville: Thomas Nelson, 1994), 70.

7. Zachary Crockett, "The Economics of All-You-Can-Eat Buffets," *The Hustle*, January 25, 2020, https://thehustle.co/the-economics-of-all-you-can-eat-buffets.

8. On these and other questions, see Rick Warren's *Dynamic Bible Study Methods* (Wheaton: Victor, 1989).

9. William Martin, *A Prophet with Honor: The Billy Graham Story* (New York: Harper, 1992), 112.

10. Martin, *A Prophet with Honor.*

Chapter 3 Talking to God

1. C. S. Lewis, *Letters to Malcolm, Chiefly on Prayer* (New York: Harcourt, 1964), 57.

2. On this, see Jeremias, *The Prayers of Jesus*, 96. Talmudic reference: *b.Ber.* 40a (Bar.) par *b. Sanh.* 70b (bar.).

3. As Tony Campolo has joked; Tony Campolo, *You Can Make a Difference* (Waco: Word, 1984), 116.

4. C. S. Lewis, *The Screwtape Letters* (New York: Bantam, 1982), xiii.

5. Anne Lamott, *Traveling Mercies: Some Thoughts on Faith* (New York: Pantheon Books, 1999), 82.

6. These four responses are not original with me. They have been bandied about in multiple settings and writings for some time. They were most popularized by Bill Hybels in his book *Too Busy Not to Pray*, but even there, he mentions borrowing them from another pastor. So while not original with me, I do not know their original source.

7. John Ortberg, *If You Want to Walk on Water You've Got to Get Out of the Boat* (Grand Rapids: Zondervan, 2014), 91–93.

Chapter 4 Spending Time with God

1. I am not sure from where (or whom) I first began thinking of this scene from the life of Jesus as a model for our time with God, coupled with the impact it can have on our own, but I am relatively confident that it is not wholly original with me.

2. Thomas R. Kelly, *A Testament of Devotion* (New York: Harper and Row, 1941).

3. This observation, as well as the dialogue from the movie *Nell*, is taken from Gire, *The Reflective Life*, 9–11. See also Mary Ann Evans, *Nell* (New York: Berkley Books, 1995), 243.

4. Kelly, *A Testament of Devotion*, 120.

5. John Ortberg, *The Life You've Always Wanted* (Grand Rapids: Zondervan, 1997), 70.

6. On the two levels of life, see Kelly's *A Testament of Devotion*, 35–38.

7. As quoted by MacDonald, *The Life God Blesses*, 71.

8. Adapted from Lettie Cowman, *Springs in the Valley* (Grand Rapids: Zondervan, 1939), 196–97.

9. Cowman, *Springs in the Valley*, 197.

10. Foster, *Celebration of Discipline*, 15.

11. Dietrich Bonhoeffer, *Life Together: A Discussion of Christian Fellowship* (New York: Harper and Row, 1954), 79.

12. On this, see Gire, *The Reflective Life*, 87–103.

13. Gire, *The Reflective Life*, 89.

14. On this, see the author's *Serious Times: Making Your Life Matter in an Urgent Day* (Downers Grove, IL: InterVarsity Press, 2004), 82.

15. *The Rule of St. Benedict*, ed. Timothy Fry (New York: Vintage, 1998), 3.

16. Fr. Luke Dysinger, O.S.B., "Accepting the Embrace of God: The Ancient Art of *Lectio Divina*," as offered on the St. Andrew's Abbey Homepage at http://www.valyermo.com/ld-art.html.

17. On this approach, I am indebted to the little pamphlet *Seven Minutes a Day with God*, published by NavPress.

Chapter 5 Experiencing Life in Community

1. Bonhoeffer, *Life Together*, 78.

2. Charles Stockdale, "TV Shows with the Most Emmy Wins of All Time," *USA Today*, September 11, 2018, https://usatoday.com/story/money/2018/9/11/tv-shows-with-the-most-emmy-wins-of-all-time/37351013/.

3. The *Cheers* theme song, "Where Everybody Knows Your Name," was written by Gary Portnoy and published by SONY/ATV Music.

4. See also the author's chapter on rethinking community in *Rethinking the Church* (Grand Rapids: Baker, 2003).

5. As quoted in Philip Yancey, *What's So Amazing About Grace?*, 175.

6. See the author's *Christianity for People Who Aren't Christians* and *The Rise of the Nones* (Grand Rapids: Baker, 2014).

7. Henry Cloud, *Changes That Heal* (New York: Harper, 1995), 55.

8. Adapted from John R. W. Stott, *Christian Basics* (Grand Rapids: Baker, 1991), 128.

9. This is not original with me—if my memory serves, it comes from my friend Rick Warren.

10. Charles Colson, *The Body* (Dallas: Word, 1992), 131.

11. This story has been adapted from an address given by Henry Cloud; see also his book *Safe People* (Grand Rapids: Zondervan, 1995), 157.

12. Bonhoeffer, *Life Together*, 19.

13. Lamott, *Traveling Mercies*, 55.

14. Adapted from John Maxwell, *The Winning Attitude* (San Bernardino, CA: Here's Life, 1984), 76, emphasis added.

15. Maxwell, *The Winning Attitude*, 50–51.

16. Adapted from Gordon MacDonald, *Restoring Your Spiritual Passion* (Nashville: Oliver-Nelson Books, 1986), 71–91.

17. Much of my thinking on mentoring is owed to Paul Stanley and his book *Connecting* (Colorado Springs: NavPress, 1992).

Chapter 6 Worshiping in Spirit and Truth

1. Leland Ryken, *Redeeming the Time* (Grand Rapids: Baker Books, 1995), 12.

2. Ryken, *Redeeming the Time*.

3. Foster, *Celebration of Discipline*, 148.

4. See Romans 6:1–11.

5. See Matthew 3:16, which references Jesus "coming up out" of the water.

6. See "Baptism, Wash" by G. R. Beasley-Murray in *The New International Dictionary of New Testament Theology*, vol. 1, edited by Colin Brown (Grand Rapids: Zondervan, 1986), 1:143–61.

7. For background information on Christian baptism, see G. R. Beasley-Murray, *Baptism in the New Testament* (Grand Rapids: Eerdmans, 1962); Oscar Cullman, *Baptism in the New Testament* (Philadelphia: Westminster Press, 1950); along with the excellent chapter on baptism found in Ralph Martin's *The Worship of God* (Grand Rapids: Eerdmans, 1982), 124–44.

8. For background information on the Lord's Supper, see C. K. Barrett, *Church, Ministry, and Sacraments in the New Testament* (Grand Rapids: Eerdmans, 1985); Markus Barth, *Rediscovering the Lord's Supper* (Atlanta: John Knox, 1988); along with the excellent overview given by Ralph Martin in *The Worship of God*, 145–70.

Chapter 7 Becoming a Player

1. J. R. R. Tolkien, *The Fellowship of the Ring* (New York: Houghton Mifflin Company, 1996), 319.

2. Charles R. Swindoll, *Improving Your Serve* (Nashville: W. Publishing Group, 1981), 43–44.

3. "Human Genome Project," Wikipedia.org, accessed January 2020, https://en.wikipedia.org/wiki/Human_Genome_Project.

4. Rick Warren, *The Purpose Driven Life* (Grand Rapids: Zondervan, 2012).

5. The four lists are found in Romans 12, 1 Corinthians 12, Ephesians 4, and 1 Peter 4.

6. For example, our church has a spiritual gifts assessment test offered online at Mecklenburg.org/serve.

7. Stephen Pile, *The (Incomplete) Book of Failures: The Official Handbook of the Not-Terribly-Good Club of Great Britain* (Boston: E. P. Dutton, 1979).

8. Henri J. M. Nouwen, *The Wounded Healer: Ministry in Contemporary Society* (New York: Image Books, 1979).

9. Jim Collins, *Good to Great: Why Some Companies Make the Leap and Others Don't* (New York: HarperCollins, 2001).

10. To go further with this, see Gordon MacDonald's *Ordering Your Private World* (Chicago: Moody, 1984); Charles Hummel's *Freedom from Tyranny of the Urgent* (Downers Grove: InterVarsity, 1997); and Richard Swenson's *Margin* (Colorado Springs: NavPress, 1992).

11. Anthony Campolo, *Who Switched the Price Tags?* (Nashville: Word, 1986), 117–18. See also M. Scott Peck, *The Road Less Traveled* (New York: Touchstone, 1978).

12. Adapted from Tom Rath, *StrengthsFinder 2.0* (New York: Simon and Schuster, 2007), 29.

Chapter 8 Positioning Your Heart

1. Anne Tergesen, "Want to Reach Your Savings Goal in 2020? Here's What the Research Says Will Help," *The Wall Street Journal*, December 26, 2019, https://www.wsj.com/articles/want-to-reach-your-savings-goal-in-2020-heres-what-the-research-says-will-help-11577356205.

2. Joe Pinsker, "It Isn't the Kids. It's the Cost of Raising Them," *The Atlantic*, February 27, 2019, https://www.theatlantic.com/family/archive/2019/02/cost-rais ing-kids-parents-happiness/583699/.

3. "Divorce Study: Financial Arguments Early in Relationship May Predict Divorce," *Huffington Post*, July 12, 2013, https://www.huffpost.com/entry/divorce -study_n_3587811.

4. John S. Kiernan, "40 Million People Say They'll Miss at Least One Credit Card Due Date in 2019," *WalletHub*, February 19, 2019, https://wallethub.com /blog/late-payments-survey/58680/.

5. Zack Friedman, "78% of Workers Live Paycheck to Paycheck," *Forbes*, January 11, 2019, https://www.forbes.com/sites/zackfriedman/2019/01/11/live -paycheck-to-paycheck-government-shutdown/#6bfe0fc44f10.

6. David Bach, *The Latte Factor* (New York: Atria Books, 2019).

7. Jennifer Liu, "Why Americans Can't Keep Lifestyle Spending in Check," AOL, May 20, 2015, https://www.aol.com/article/finance/2015/05/20/why-amer icans-cant-keep-lifestyle-spending-in-check/21185508/.

8. "Millennials Are Spending More Money on Coffee Than Retirement Plans," Fox News, January 18, 2017, https://www.foxnews.com/food-drink/millennials -are-spending-more-money-on-coffee-than-retirement-plans.

9. Bill Fay, "Key Figures Behind America's Consumer Debt," Debt.org, https://www.debt.org/faqs/americans-in-debt/.

10. U. S. and World Population Clock, US Census Bureau, https://www.cen sus.gov/popclock/.

11. Fay, "Key Figures."

12. "Average Credit Card Interest Rates (APR)," ValuePenguin, accessed January 2020, https://www.valuepenguin.com/average-credit-card-interest-rates.

Chapter 9 Achieving Maximum Impact

1. Penn Jillette, "Penn Says: A Gift of a Bible," YouTube, July 8, 2010, https://www.youtube.com/watch?v=6md638smQd8&t=5s.

2. "Almost Half of Practicing Christian Millennials Say Evangelism Is Wrong," *Barna*, February 5, 2019, https://www.barna.com/research/millennials-oppose-evangelism/.

3. I am indebted to Bill Hybels for my overall treatment of this text.

4. I am not sure where I first heard it coined this way, but I'm confident it is not original with me.

5. Adapted from Ken Gire, *Seeing What Is Sacred* (Nashville: W Publishing Group, 2006),188–90.

6. Excerpt from Samuel Shoemaker's poem "I Stand by the Door" from *I Stand by the Door: The Life of Sam Shoemaker* by Helen Smith Shoemaker. Copyright © 1967 by Helen Smith Shoemaker. Used by permission of HarperCollins Publishers.

Chapter 10 Keeping in Step

1. One of the better books on this is by John R. W. Stott, *The Baptism and Fullness of the Holy Spirit* (Downers Grove, IL: InterVarsity Press, 1971).

2. J. Robertson McQuilkin, "Living by Vows," http://www.ciu.edu/faculty-publications/article/living-vows; see also the writings of Philip Yancey on McQuilkin.

3. Robertson McQuilkin's Resignation Speech, YouTube, posted February 10, 2014, https://www.youtube.com/watch?v=MqtG-XfxMC4&feature=youtu.be.

Afterword The Committed Life

1. Dietrich Bonhoeffer, *The Cost of Discipleship* (New York: Collier, 1963), 99.

2. Adapted from Bill Barnhart, "Market Report: In the Heat of Battle, Traders Rule," *Chicago Tribune*, April 25, 1994, sec. 4, p. 1.

3. Adapted from Mrs. Howard Taylor, *Borden of Yale '09: The Life That Counts* (China Inland Mission, 1927). See also *The Yale Standard*, Fall 1970 edition.

James Emery White is the founding and senior pastor of Mecklenburg Community Church and the ranked adjunctive professor of Theology and Culture at Gordon-Conwell Theological Seminary, at which he also served as the fourth president. In addition, he is a distinguished professor at Anderson University. Dr. White holds BS, MDiv, and PhD degrees involving study at Southern Seminary, Vanderbilt University, and Oxford University in England, and is the author of more than twenty books. He is the father of four and the grandfather of ten (and counting!).

Honest Answers to the Questions They're Already Asking

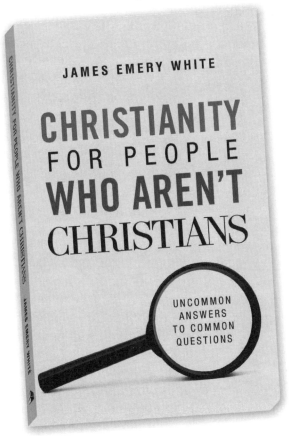

"I wish this book had been around when I was an atheist and started to seek God. It's a no-nonsense, practical, and insightful guide that will help all those on a quest for spiritual truth. If you're investigating whether there's any substance to the Christian faith, you must read this important book."

—**Lee Strobel**, former award-winning legal editor of the *Chicago Tribune* and bestselling author of more than twenty books

Welcome to the first truly
POST-CHRISTIAN GENERATION

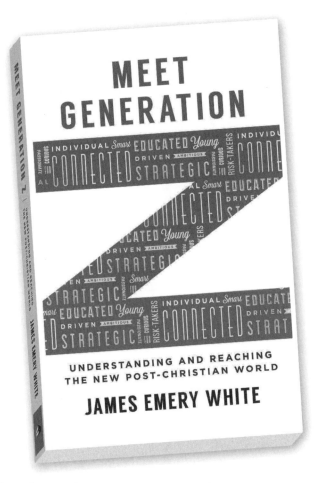

"In *Meet Generation Z*, James Emery White shares helpful insights into the generation that follows the millennial generation in a clear, practical way. Pastors and church leaders seeking to better understand the world of their youth ought to read this text."

—**Ed Stetzer**, Billy Graham Distinguished Chair, Wheaton College

ALSO BY
JAMES EMERY WHITE

James Emery White lends his prophetic voice to one of the most important conversations the church needs to have today. He calls churches to examine their current methods of evangelism, which often result only in transfer growth—Christians moving from one church to another—rather than in reaching the "nones."

BakerBooks
a division of Baker Publishing Group
www.BakerBooks.com

Available wherever books and ebooks are sold.

Explore
ChurchandCulture.org

BLOG | HEADLINE NEWS | RESOURCES